NEIGHBORHOOD VOICES

NEIGHBORHOOD VOICES

Edited by D.L. Ware

Presented by Literary Cleveland and
Cleveland Public Library

First Edition 2021
ISBN: 978-1-950843-37-4

PARAFINE PRESS

Parafine Press
5322 Fleet Avenue, Cleveland, Ohio 44105
www.parafinepress.com
Cover and book design by Meredith Pangrace

Neighborhood Voices is a city-wide creative writing project designed by Literary Cleveland and the Cleveland Public Library to engage writers across Cleveland, allowing residents to connect with neighbors, share stories of their community, and draft new writing about what makes their neighborhood unique. To learn more, visit the online version of this anthology at *voices.cpl.org*.

This collection
is a gathered voice
that catches rich cultural
and heritage,
gets the diversity
in experience
in this time, in our place.
in this shared space,
we sing this city in unison.

CONTENTS

IV. OUR NEIGHBORHOODS ARE MORE THAN HOME

V. CLEVELAND IS WHERE WE LIVE REGARDLESS

VI. PARTS OF A WHOLE CITY

VII. CLEVELAND IS WHAT WE OFFER IN OUR WORDS

Introduction: Voices of the Chorus

Neighborhood Voices is a citywide creative writing project designed by Literary Cleveland and the Cleveland Public Library to engage writers across the city of Cleveland, allowing residents to connect with neighbors, share stories of their community, and draft new writing about what makes their neighborhood unique. Between June and July 2020, free writing workshops were held online via Zoom (due to COVID-19) in six different regions of the city, with each workshop facilitated by a different teaching artist: Darlene Montonaro, Philip Metres, Jason Harris, me (D.L. Ware), Vince Robinson, and Stephanie Ginese. At the end of the summer, we received submissions from more than eighty residents all across the city and collected their poems, essays, and memoirs into this anthology showcasing the vibrant lives and voices in Cleveland neighborhoods.

In the pages that follow, you will find the selected submissions of the literary artist that stayed true to form, where their words and phrases add texture and history to an already written Cleveland landscape. These writers and poets selflessly share themselves in the telling of their triumphs, tragedies, and the moments they remember as Clevelanders.

In Karen Gygli's "Collinwood Stories, Told and Untold," she remembers the bombing of Danny Green's apartment on Waterloo as she reimagines the 1970s gothic soap opera *Dark Shadows* with Barnabas the vampire. In Sonya Pryor-Jones's poetic prose "I Think I'm Missing Glenville," she speaks on how the old Glenville is reminiscent of her late grandmother and how she has vowed to return home. The poetry of Glenville's Anita Tobin, by way of Austin, Texas, shares her love and vision of her hometown. In the poem "Cleveland 2050," she writes the prophetic lines "We will be the free radicals / As we approach the precipice / New age mentality . . . " Lisa Chiu's "Can Understand, Cannot Speak" reveals the history of our Asiatown and her experience as a waitress in the 1980s. This *Neighborhood Voices Anthology* provided a platform for Cleveland-based writers to contribute their voice as the chorus of this literary city.

From the seasoned poetic work of Ray McNiece's "Ode to Lake Erie" to Bruce Checefsky's walk through "Hough," as the reader you are now in the possession of Cleveland's most formidable memories, rhythmic lines of poetry, and serious analytics about the issues that impacted our lives in our neighborhoods daily. From the Lee-Harvard community to

West Park, we share our voice, hoping that you view our beloved city through the lens of resilience and unity, not the inaccurate mechanism of measurements, collected data, and the impersonal national reports used to tear us down and keep us divided. This manuscript sings the songs of stories made of immigrants and new beginnings, the uncertainties of COVID-19 and its ever-changing circumstances, stories of togetherness and work ethic in concert with Cleveland's cultural heritage and the spirit of the working class that is still alive herein.

Cleveland writes itself in a universal language, breaking down the barriers, the gaps, the dissolution about who we are and what it means to be a proud Clevelander. Read how the differences that surround us transform into the complexities of our diverse city. Hear how the words written give context to the beauty of Tremont, the history of St. Clair, and the creativity of Gordon Square. Reflect upon the better days, as our essays and memoirs connect us all, in examining what has happened to Glenville or what is going on in Mt. Pleasant on Miles and Union. Feel the humor and the elegant poetic verses with its chiseled stanzas bring attention and awareness to the challenges and the dangers that lurk in Detroit-Shoreway, on Kinsman, and around Downtown. Participate in the unearthing of the lesser known histories and facts and explore the found inspirations of Buckeye, Larchmere, and East 55th as it reminds us how the old and the new are interconnected.

We sing the song of Cleveland as the voices of this chorus, and as a community of writers we celebrate the very things that make us strong, worthy, and unique through technique, genre, and imagination.

And as your composers, we leave small ambitious pieces of ourselves here in, laid out to be read and referred to forever, as representatives of what makes this city so great.

—Poet D. L. Ware

I. CLEVELAND IS A BLOODLINE

My Home with Love

TONEISHA BLACK (Hough)

CLE I say that city proud
Forever my home since '97
Who knew I was born in the best city
No boasting just toasting
To a home that's just over near Hough
Growing up and feeling like I'm in a mystical place
Imperfectly perfect I would call it
Protected in a generational three-story home
On a little street called Holyrood
Where growing up I made friends that
In turn created memories
Playing in the big huge field across the street
Enjoying the company of the elders watching over
It's here where I experience my first blackout in '03
Hot and only small
Scared and not knowing
While the candles flicker
And the real heat outside had temperatures rising
Oh and minds going crazy
But what was fun was school
John W. Raper
I met my real best friend
I met a sister
I met wonderful teachers
Cleveland in my eyes
A very big treasure
Talent and really bright
Jamming out to the block parties every summer
Can't forget the huge Hough Parade
In the dead heat of summer playing around or handling my business on the Daughters of the Nile
Proudly stomping my feet and yelling to the beat
Now I may have moved on
But not too far away

From the place that's shaped me
From the beautiful history it brings
Even though some things crashed and burned
Its memory is imprinted
The revision for the better
Cleveland my dear city
On that little street I told you guys about
In that three-story home filled with memories
That's where I am from

Paper Airplanes

GEOFFREY POLK (Kinsman)

At Alexander Hamilton Junior High between Kinsman and Union
I kept getting sent out of class and didn't know why.
I played by the rules like the rest of the assembly line
stamping out our passing grades, course by tedious course.
My face must have been an open book, diffident,
outraged when the teacher put a block of wood
under Deborah Glaefke's chair to keep her legs
from swinging all day as she looked out the window—
of course she became a poet I later learned.
I watched her pale legs under her plaid skirt
as the math teacher explained how to get from point A to B
but I hadn't started at A and I didn't want their B.
I didn't have words for what I wanted.

They sent me to the book room, narrow and cramped,
textbooks piled to the ceiling in double-helix stacks
on the verge of falling. My duties undefined, I sat guardian
over the unwanted texts, paging through the stamped
checkout boxes, tripping over names from the past,
Stephen Shipley and Susan Schbrowski. I read randomly,
like a dust filter we should have all been issued
going from peeling rental to peeling schoolhouse
but instead of lead I caught stray facts and fiction
as they floated and drifted in the stifling air over the musty books—
Newton and dinosaurs, T. S. Eliot and suffragettes.

The deeply grained split door scraped open behind me
as a codefendant was shepherded into the room.
We looked at each other awkwardly as I tried
to explain our function, embarrassed to say we had none,
but soon I'd enlist him in an airplane throwing contest.
I had jury-rigged a fragile stairway up the books
and across shelves to a small high window.
From our perch, hunched between sill and shelf

we folded planes from yellowed mimeographs
and launched them from our third-floor height.
They sailed gloriously through the Indian summer wind
landing on roofs and cars like freak snow
and on the sidewalk where I hoped someone
from the other side of where we were
would pick them up, look up at the brick walls and see
in the paper planes a sign, a desire to escape, a chance.

Case Study 1968

MARK GILSON (University Circle)

I never went to Case Western Reserve in University Circle. But my girlfriend did. This is how we got acquainted in August 1968.

The US Junior Chess Open was held at Case Western Reserve that year, and our Latvian chess coach insisted we go. It was an hour's journey from Perry in eastern Lake County, so we stayed at the dormitory on campus and competed in Thwing Hall. Twenty-one years prior, the tournament had been won by an upstart named Bobby Fischer. For a prize, they gave him a portable typewriter. We were high school juniors from a small town, and this was quite an adventure. Anything seemed possible. There were ninety-two competitors from across the country with four in our own group—three boys, one girl, with no chaperone.

We had quite a chess club in tiny Perry. A year later, we would place second at the state team championship for high schools. But in this tournament, up against the top young players from across the country, we were taking our lumps. The tournament lasted four days, but chess became a lesser highlight. There was a Howard Johnson's on Euclid across from Wade Park and the Holy Oil Can, and that's where we went for black fudge sundaes. The days were consumed with chess, but in the evenings we were on our own. The Republican National Convention was going on and, being wonky kids, that's what we watched in the TV room of the dormitory. There were Rockefellers and Romneys in the mix as thousands of convention-goers in Miami waved signs and stayed up past their bedtime. On the second night of our tournament, she and I outlasted the others in the TV room and somewhere between the failed nominations of Howard Stassen and Ohio Governor Jim Rhodes, we hugged and began a four-year on-again, off-again relationship. I did not excel at chess that week, but I always thought I fared better than America, which ended up with Richard Nixon and Spiro T. Agnew.

By the next evening, because of my new friendship, I became the object of ridicule among my roommates. They took my Hai Karate aftershave (I had no reason to own aftershave) and threw it around the room, breaking it against a wall. We all reeked of Hai Karate. Then they kidnapped me, ostensibly to see *Chitty Chitty Bang Bang* at the Hippodrome downtown. Our female competitor declined, or was not invited, I cannot remember, but what we ended up seeing was *2001: A Space Odyssey* by Stanley Kubrick, a life-changing experience in itself. We were a bunch of out-of-town kids traveling the nighttime sidewalks and buses of Euclid, but we never once worried about our safety.

She and I had lunch one day at an Italian place on Euclid Avenue near Little Italy. It may have been called the Aurora Room. She was small and perky. At one point she put her hand to her chin and leaned her elbow on the edge of the small round table, tipping it, and sending the salt and pepper shakers to the floor along with the parmesan cheese. Ultimately, during that week, she became the US Junior Woman's Champion.

After high school, she went to Case Western Reserve, and I went to Ohio State. I visited her whenever I could get home. We loved movies and plays in the grand theaters around town, staying out late. Many times, I thundered home along Liberty Boulevard (soon renamed MLK) in my parents' Dodge Monaco station wagon with imitation wood panels on the side. For several years, University Circle became the cradle that nurtured us. Not far from the Hough riots in 1966 and the Glenville shootout in the summer of 1968, we took quiet walks around the campus and Wade Park. The guards at the Cleveland Botanical Garden ushered us out for smooching more than once. (Unlike the Vietnam War that was going on at the time, there was very little escalation in our relationship.) She became an usher for the Cleveland Orchestra and got me into Severance Hall for free. We haunted the art museum.

Despite the chaos and suffering and violence going on around us, it was a magical time in Cleveland. We saw Simon and Garfunkel at a sold-out Public Hall. There was a fancy restaurant atop a tall motel on the Shoreway where we stopped for ice cream after dates. We competed in many tournaments at the Cleveland Chess Club in the attic of the giant Masonic Temple near Euclid and East 40th.

Eventually, sadly, inevitably, we drifted apart, married others, moved on to different all-consuming lives. She became a vegetarian and a Buddhist. I became a Republican, but once demonstrated against Spiro T. Agnew when he visited Columbus. Perhaps it was the chess experiences, but we both became CPAs and worked downtown for major firms at various points. We met for lunch once at Earth by April, a vegetarian place out by Cedar and Lee. Even today, we continue to correspond, although neither of us visit our chess boards very often.

We grew up and Cleveland grew up in unpredictable ways. Life intervenes.

Years later, still living in Perry thirty-five miles to the east, my wife and I enjoyed special evenings at Top-of-the-Town at Erieview, the Watermark and Sammy's in the East Flats. We miss the New York Spaghetti House on East 9th and Frank's Frontier Restaurant on East 13th. We have watched and participated in the rebirth of Playhouse Square. Sadly, the grand old Hippodrome Theater on Euclid Avenue was eventually knocked down for a parking lot.

Do the downtowners realize how important Cleveland is for all of us in Northeastern Ohio?

We are all Clevelanders. We all share in the joys and the magic and the sorrows of this vital nexus. Our city remains a place for hallowed memories, countless lives and loves, as new generations forge fresh connections and limitless dreams.

hot soup on a cool late-summer evening

JEFFREY BOWEN (Edgewater)

made with love and tenderness
from locally grown zucchini,
bright yellow sweet corn,
fresh cut basil,
sliced into aromatic ribbons,
and lush roma tomatoes
from the west side market.

there is also artisan-crafted sourdough bread,
straight from the hearth fire,
dipped slowly into extra virgin olive oil,
seasoned carefully with dark green rosemary
and pink himalayan sea salt
from urban herbs,

plus a hearty salad of locally sourced
microgreens from
community greenhouse partners,
tossed gently,
with shredded carrots,
and chopped red cabbage
from the tremont farmer's market
and a dash of balsamic vinegar.

this delectable,
culinary treat
was packed with love
by a kindred spirit,
who sent me reeling
into early evening sunshine,
after a delightful day of
working together

in the garden,
and a morning of sweet kisses,
homemade banana bread,
and rich black phoenix coffee,
ground by hand
and prepared
with meditative care.

it is also very much
worth noting,
that the seasonal
ohio peaches
are sweeter than ever,
and as juicy as can be.

My West Side Story

PAUL KOSZKALDA (Detroit-Shoreway)

I was born in May 1958 at the old St. John Hospital located on Detroit Avenue at West 79th. I was the first born to my parents Pete and Mary. My brother Bob came along in September 1960. We lived in a double house on West 69th just south of Bridge Avenue. Old West High was across the street a couple hundred feet north. My paternal grandparents lived downstairs and we lived upstairs. My dad was a machinist who was born in Ukraine. He and his family came to the USA in 1949. My mom was your typical stay-at-home mom in my younger years. She was born on Detroit Avenue at West 57th in the family apartment above a hardware store. They met when my dad's family moved into the house on West 69th. My mom lived next door. Backyard romance. They were married in 1957. I lived in that house until 1988. My dad lived there until 2002.

Today they call my old neighborhood Detroit-Shoreway, but back in the 1960s it was just the Near West Side. It was a solid middle-class neighborhood of single and double houses on postage-stamp-size city lots. The area was safe and clean. I must say it was a little rough around the edges. It got rougher as the years went on. The areas south of Madison Avenue and east of West 58th were showing signs of decline and becoming more than rough around the edges. The main intersection of the neighborhood was and still is Detroit and West 65th, also known as Gordon Square. We never called it that back then. It was rather seedy even back then, not dangerous until later years. But it had its share of bums and winos as they were called then. Gordon Square was home to a variety of businesses. I'll address that in more detail later. As for my immediate neighborhood, we had a mix of ethnic groups. We had a large number of Italians, Puerto Ricans, Irish and hillbillies. Yes, hillbillies. That's what they called themselves, and they were proud to be called that. So, we had a nice mix. It was the middle of the baby boom, so the area was teaming with kids. I recently wrote down a list of kids I could remember and the list numbered eighty within maybe three or four blocks. Because there were so many kids, there was always somebody to play with. It was a great place to grow up.

SCHOOL DAYS

I attended Lawn Elementary School on Lawn Avenue around West 74th from 1963 to 1970. Kids on my street that lived south of Bridge went to Lawn, those north went to Watterson. The Catholic kids went to St. Colman or St. Stephen. I walked to school. It took about ten minutes. There was always a group of kids that walked together. On the way we would walk across the West 74th Street bridge which was above the railroad and rapid tracks. South of Madison there was an asphalt playground just before reaching the school. The playground sparkled in the sun because of the thousands of shards of broken glass. Lawn was in that rougher area I mentioned before.

Lawn was built about 1902. Due to the baby boom, an addition was added when I was in second grade. Most kids went home for lunch at noon and returned to school by 1:15. A few kids stayed for lunch and ate their homemade lunch on some tables on the third floor. In my later years at Lawn, I delivered milk to classrooms for morning snacks. I also ran the movie projector. Anything to get out of class, all under the guise of providing service.

A few notable things: A boy named Jimmy lived four houses from me. He was very smart but didn't have a lick of sense. He was always bucking heads with the other kids especially on the way to and from school. He would often report us to the principal. We'd get called into the office and even Jimmy's sister would stick up for us. Once on the way home from school, he was chasing one of us and fell into the street on the bridge. He just missed getting hit by a car. Cruel kids that we were, we all cheered for him to get hit. Close call.

There was a boy named William in my class. He'd walk with us part of the way home. William was a bit on the rowdy side. He used to find bricks in the lot next to the Rapid tracks and wait for the Rapid to come by and drop the bricks onto the train cars. I never did that, but I did enjoy watching him. If William or Jimmy weren't up to their tricks, the walk was uneventful. On the way home, we would pass the West High kids coming home in the opposite direction. A few times in 1970, we would hear about sit-ins and protests in the West. It was the height of the Vietnam war era, just before Kent State.

Jimmy's cousin Mike was my best friend back then, we would watch the cars go by on our walk to school and call out the model and year.

For junior high, I went to West Junior High, which was the aforementioned West High. Built in 1902, it was a high school until

September 1970 when I started there. Old West High merged with Old Lincoln High to become Lincoln-West High. The old building became the junior high.

Living across the street from school meant I could sleep later. A nice perk. I had a lunch pass, so I came home for lunch because I lived close. Most kids ate in the cafeteria. Some kids would cut school and hang out on our front porch. My grandfather would have to chase them away. He only spoke Ukrainian, but the kids got the point. Most of the time. One time the kids weren't cooperative, so he brought out a pistol. I was upstairs eating lunch. I knew what was going on and was very worried about what might happen. Nothing did. The kids left probably in fear for their lives. The old man with a pistol had the upper hand.

In seventh grade, the girls walked out demanding to be allowed to wear pants or jeans. The school gave in.

I went to West Tech for high school. I just loved those three years. What a great school. Tech would vie for largest school in Ohio with Lakewood High. No doubt it was the best high school in the system before the school system went to crap. I took vocational drafting and had a job before graduating. The vocational classes always had a long list of employers waiting for the next class to graduate so they could hire the graduates. So-called progress messed that up, and that benefit eventually faded away. In 1995, the Cleveland school board closed West Tech just after spending hundreds of thousands of dollars to install new boilers. Now the building is West Tech Lofts. I still do drafting as a job. It's on a computer. Now it's called CAD.

PLAY TIME

During the summer, we played baseball on the West High football practice field. Someone would go around house to house and recruit kids to play. This started about 10 a.m., and we would play until dark with a break for dinner. It was very much like the movie *The Sandlot*. We almost always had enough players. How we played all day without the water bottles kids today have to play sports, I don't know. Sometimes we would collect pop bottles left on the ground and turn them in at Joe's Store across from my house. At the time, you would get a penny or two as a refund for returning bottles. If we collected enough, we could buy a pop—twelve cents for twelve ounces or sixteen cents for sixteen ounces. We would all drink from the same bottle making sure to wipe the top with our sweaty, dirty shirts before drinking. Sometimes we took turns drinking from somebody's garden hose. No sanitizing. Somehow, we all lived.

We sometimes played games versus the Puerto Ricans kids. They called their team the Cepedas after Orlando Cepeda, the Giants' and Cardinals' star player from Puerto Rico. These kids were dressed in the latest fashion to play ball. Fancy shirts, pants and shoes. Bright colors, green, purple and orange. The rest of us wore t-shirts, shorts and tennis shoes.

If it rained and the field was muddy, we played basketball in the school parking lot.

We played football in the fall on the grass on the West 69th side of the school.

The school was great for playing Army. There were window wells outside of the basement classrooms that made great trenches or bunkers. We played World War II despite the fact the current war was in Vietnam.

We played lots of tag at West usually after it got dark and could not play sports. Once some Italian kids decided to play firecracker tag. I opted out of that dangerous game. We also played a game similar to tag where we would hide a plastic baseball bat. The kid who found the bat would get to chase the others back to the base while whacking them with the bat below the waist. I was slow so I took a beating. During the summer we often didn't get inside until close to 11 p.m. We had no worries about being out that late and neither did our parents.

We played lots of board games on various porches. At one house, we played 45 rpm records in the basement. "Hanky Panky" by Tommy James and the Shondells was a favorite, as was "Let's Hang On" by the Four Seasons. The Irish and Italian kids both were big Four Seasons fans, as am I. At that same house, there was a large tree in the middle of the back yard that kept the grass from growing. We would use popsicle sticks to build roads in the dirt for our toy cars. There was an Italian family next to me. They always had a nice garden, and they also had a wine press in the basement. We were in the basement playing a board game with the TV on in the background when word came that Dr. Martin Luther King Jr. had been shot.

I must add that none of this playing involved play dates scheduled by our moms. No juice boxes and no prepackaged snacks. It was a wonderful time and place to be a kid.

OTHER THINGS

Joe's Store also made pizza for a while. It was your usual mom-and-pop corner store. I sometimes would go across to the store between innings of the Indians game I was watching and get an RC Cola and a bag of chips and return before the next inning started. My parents would send me or Bob over for a carton of cigarettes or a case of Stroh's beer. Mind you, we were elementary school age at the time. Over the years the store changed hands, always to Italian owners. One summer they installed a bocce ball court on the side of the store, complete with lights. That made for great entertainment. We'd watch as they argued in Italian.

There was a Pick-n-Pay grocery store at West 65th and Franklin. My mom would send Bob and me there before we went out to play to get bread, milk and other items. Pick-n-Pay replaced a funeral home. The Rite-Aid drug store is there now.

The other three corners of that intersection had gas stations. Shell, Sohio (now BP), and Union 76. We filled our bicycle tires at the Shell station.

There was a Lawson's convenience store at West 58th and Bridge, later they put one at West 74th and Franklin. It is still a store called The Deli.

At the south end of our street were the railroad and Rapid tracks. There was an abandoned railroad siding. The family that lived on the corner would put on a massive firework show there on July 4th. A little farther down that street was a small playground we would go to. For a couple of summers, I think 1970 and '71, the kids in my neighborhood were provided free lunches every weekday at the playground. I remember the baloney sandwiches with butter in particular. One negative thing about living so close to the Rapid was you could hear the first train of the morning. That was a warning it was almost time to wake up for school or, in later years, work. Other times of the day I never really noticed the sound of the trains, just at the break of day.

I remember high school kids burning rubber in their hot rods in front of my house after school. Skid marks were everywhere. Rear wheel drive. West 69th was a brick street until the summer of 1968 when the city paved it with asphalt. The band room at West High was the nearest to my house. We could hear the bands practice during the warm weather months when the windows were open.

So, it was fun growing up on West 69th. I have lots of good memories. Sleeping on the porch in the summer was great. Going to fires in the middle of the night like when Waverly school burned only to find all of your friends there too. That was kind of weird.

Our Lady of Mt. Carmel festival was my favorite summer event. I still go there. We'd walk down there and hang out on the midway. Each day they would shoot off a couple of fireworks at the start of the festival. We could hear the festival's Italian band from my house. We could also hear the rock bands at Edgewater park for WIXY 1260 Appreciation days. Labor Day weekend meant I could watch the jets fly over the house.

Gordon Square was the hub of the area. There was a drugstore where the coffee shop is on the southeast corner. The Capitol Theatre showed international films. The Arcade building had a dime store, a liquor store and barbershop. Upstairs where doctors and dentists' offices. There were a few greasy spoon restaurants like Perry's. Numerous bars like the City Grill and Yankee Bar, rather slimy establishments. Pioneer Savings and a few other banks. The Romanian and Russian churches, a couple of bakeries and funeral homes too. Little by little the area went into decline. Part of the front cornice of the Gordon Square Arcade fell onto the sidewalk. There was serious talk the building might be demolished. Fortunately, it was saved and rehabbed.

LAST WORD

As for my street, West Junior High was demolished in 1975 and replaced with a fortress-like modern building. The new building was originally called West Junior High; the name was actually on the building. The name was suddenly changed to Joseph M. Gallagher after a long-time school board member. The school board left the site of the old building pretty much in a neglected state for a couple of years. Each year just before Election Day, whether for board members or a school levy, construction equipment would suddenly appear only to disappear after the election. How curious! Eventually they built a track and a pitiful baseball diamond on the sight. About the same time the condition of the houses began to decline as older residents died off and a poorer population moved in. Property was not maintained. The area became unsafe. The decline continued for decades. Now the situation is improving. Properties are being rehabilitated including the house I grew up in.

Moribund Bijou

DENISE MONIQUE (Glenville)

It's Thursday at 12 p.m. and the sun is singing, "Hello Denise!" My black suitcase from Marc's is packed and in my trunk, and I am ready to roll. My husband, sons, and I are headed to Williamstown, Kentucky, to avoid the Fourth of July here. Here, where there are just as many fields as there are houses. Signs of alcohol sales illuminate the stores windows. A disheveled man asks for money as I wait for the traffic light to change. Glenville—once a thriving community reduced to survival. The gloom around me increases my desire to escape. We have a weekend planned of fishing, playing Mega Bloks, and enjoying ourselves. I have completed my master's degree and deserve peace. Oh, how I live for our getaways!

Sometimes, in my community, I feel like I am a yellow feather among cactus. I want to soar and enjoy life amidst the chaos all around me. My husband prays for a safe trip as we exit the driveway. A Whodini song radiates the car speakers as our three-year old son recites his ABCs. Three hours later, he is still reciting his ABCs. His voice resembles a melodic bird. I glance at my husband and notice he has drawn a picture of me on his doodle board. I feel such joy in the moment! Relishing bluegill fishing, mesmerized by the blue sky as I am stretched out in my tent. Should I move to the country?

The return home prompts an exit onto MLK Boulevard and down the side street. I fixate my eyes on the first boarded up home. Why did the person write his gang name so largely on it? Don't my neighbors have cars? If so, why am I haphazardly avoiding broken glass. Is that guy going to shoot? Why doesn't someone do something! Living in my community has plastered the significance of deciphering between fireworks and gunshots. Living in my community has taught me to use multiple locks on my doors and survey which window can safely permit a summer's breeze while keeping an intruder out. It can be a prison, yet I have not committed a crime.

Yet, if you shift your lens and slow down, just a bit, you just may find enjoyment looking at the community gardens in this lead paint filled food dessert. I immediately notice the meticulous lawn and shiny beige paint on a particular house. The patio furniture looks inviting, and I wonder who lives in this gem amid Glenville. Even during the transition, new construction brings homes to the neighborhood. Businesses take their chances in Glenville, as they open on East 105th. Some mornings, when all is quiet, I ride my bike down on East Boulevard. I watch my neighbor pull weeds from her yard as her grandson loads the grill with charcoal for their family gathering. She yells to me that she has my mail, and I say thanks. She has lived in this community for over fifty years. A man walks his dog and asks how my day is going. I once stopped my car to let the teens retrieve their basketball that had rolled in front of it. The makeshift hoop did not bother me, as they could have been doing something negative. This is Glenville—a community that has seen wealth and despair. A community that has watched banks leave, churches downsize, and people move into the suburbs. A community that has limited recreation for youth.

Glenville, the community that once drew people from all over for its beauty. Its flames have gone out. There is little sense of a community, but this is still my community. It holds the church where I was baptized. The Cultural Gardens welcome people from all over. Lake Erie is a short drive away, connecting us to Canada. Some of my neighbors remember the old Glenville and keep the same standards of respect. Others live for the moment. Creators of their own venom. Familiar faces decrease. Gentrification. What is the answer?

Everyone's Welcome Here

DOMINIC MATTHEWS (Ohio City)

A sea of parking lots and a lone tall building stranded in between. This was my first impression of the United States as I touched down at JFK Airport. When I made my way to upstate New York for grad school, taking up residence in a neighborhood 9,000 miles away from India in "the Land" was the furthest thing on my mind.

My first introduction to Cleveland was through the eyes of Norman Krumholz and John Forester. Their book *Making Equity Planning Work* was course material for a class that Forester led at planning school. However, it was not until I arrived in Cleveland did I understand the influence of Krumholz on an entire generation of city planners, community activists, and practitioners. Their book gave me a glimpse into the politics, the intrigue, and, most importantly, the community that shaped the city.

On my first night in the city, I remember walking up to the roof of the Cleveland Hostel and taking in the skyline. It was appropriate that my first interaction in the city be at a place that brought people together. The charm of a social space, public or private, has magic in it. From riding the #22 bus and sharing space with riders to sitting on the West Side Market's mezzanine watching the rush of morning shoppers, I found joy in the small things.

Wading into the East vs. West conundrum, I picked sides with Ohio City for a West 40th Street neighborhood that is more a hidden alley than street. A community where big box modern homes with large windows are starting to outnumber the older residents, but where hopscotch patterns made of chalk on the sidewalks, used car lots and folks selling fresh farm eggs are still available in plenty. As I walk around Ohio City, I am constantly surprised by the nuggets of history I discover, the beauty from a time gone and the resurgence that pushes through the new. The architect in me feels at home in the comforting stone of the St. John's Episcopal Church or the streamlined shape of the Greyhound bus station on Chester. The city planner in me marvels at how the city changes every block, from the glitz of the University area to walking under the bridge and entering the boarded parts of East Cleveland. The tension of race that hangs as apprehensively as the Sidaway Bridge.

My romance with Cleveland as an immigrant also translated into experiences that solely belonged to me. For the longest time, the Steelyard Commons and its surrounding areas captivated me. A must-see place for visiting friends to understand Cleveland in a single visual. For me, this obvious juxtaposition of big box retail in the former LTV Steel mill site with smokestacks in the background captured the story of Cleveland. Being used to company towns in India, built on steel mills and coal mines, I've always wondered if this is a fate that awaits them in the coming years.

In my short time here, in spite of all the monikers and crime stats that go with any Cleveland conversation, I've discovered that people are ready to give without reserve. Some of my best moments in the city have been completely random. A guided tour of the towering Liberty Hill Baptist Church, once a synagogue catering to a thriving Jewish population. A stop by the abandoned Warner and Swasey Observatory followed by a ride to view reptiles of all kinds at Herps Alive, a nonprofit that looks after unwanted and neglected reptiles. Coming across the Ohio City Bicycle Cooperative in the Flats and marveling at the different ways biking can touch people's lives. The crowning moment was discovering Harvey Pekar and his comics that chronicled Cleveland through a recommendation to check out Zubal Books. What would a city be without its bookstore and neighborhood bike shops? On that note, slightly off from the Horizontal Books store in Ohio City is a huge art piece that says, "Everyone's Welcome Here." I agree!

Welcome Home

ERIN RADIGAN (Warehouse District)

The sun is just starting to appear over the Gray's Block building, like a little wave hello from Mother Nature. I walk into the kitchen as brightness shines through the old ivy-covered windows, splattering rays across my freckled face.

The room feels warm for a morning in March. I'm not exactly sure how to use the old thermostat in my apartment since I've only lived here for a week. I push the tiny brown buttons until I hear the air kick on.

I notice screams coming from West 9th Street. A girl is skipping and yelling "top o' the mornin' to ya" in a bad Irish accent. She has on a shamrock headband and tall white and green tube socks.

My friends will be here soon. I'm sure they will be wearing similar St. Patrick's Day garb; green top hats, plastic shamrock necklaces, and tank tops with "Kiss Me I'm Irish" bedazzled across the front.

I start to load the glass table with food. I place everything bagels in a woven basket, scoop globs of cream cheese in tiny glass custard cups, and stack turkey and cheese pinwheel sandwiches on a white ceramic platter. I arrange a rainbow of sliced strawberries, blueberries, and oranges on a wooden cutting board.

A pot of Phoenix coffee is brewing. I grab a mug and add a generous amount of Baileys into the dark puddle of warm chocolate, nutty-flavored liquid.

"Knock, knock!" screams Jenny, as she lets herself into the open apartment.

"This place is insane! I can't believe you found this apartment!" Jenny says as she slides into the boxy navy blue velvet chair.

"Thanks for coming!" I shout as I finish taping green streamers on the white brick wall.

All of my friends start filing through the door. They bring in bottles of Jameson, cases of White Claw, and coolers filled with green Jell-O shots.

My apartment is packed. There are probably forty people here. I don't know many of them. I know my friend Jenny and can recognize some of her friends, but most of the room looks like a pool of strangers dressed in green and white t-shirts with sparkly shamrock tattoos on their cheeks.

A guy carrying a huge black speaker over his shoulder walks in.

"Hey, I live a floor above you and thought I'd stop by. Is it cool if I plug in my speaker?" he says.

"Sure," I say as I take a sip of my Irish coffee.

He plugs in his speaker and "The Middle" by Zedd instantly starts playing. The entire apartment is singing and jumping up and down like we're in the center of a mosh pit at a music festival.

As we start to stumble out of the apartment to hit the bars and see the aftermath of the St. Patrick's Day parade, I take a step back and pause. I look at the mess of people in my Warehouse apartment.

I can't believe I live here. This is my first apartment without a roommate. This is my home. I feel part of a community. I feel like a Clevelander.

Cool Cleveland

BILL NEWBY (Cleveland)

Winter comes again—
chill breezes by the water,
gray clouds blanketing the firs,
and shadow on every path.

Soon snow will spread silence
along each street.

Sun will stay hidden
during midday dark.

We will wrap ourselves in scarves
and return home with burning cheeks
to a welcomed fire
warming our frozen thighs,
forcing steam from our jeans.

East 116th Street

KIMBERLY STEELE AKA KIM THE B-WORD POET (Near West Side)

I don't know if it's like this everywhere, but I love how one's experience of Cleveland can boil down to one street. I spent the majority of my adolescent years on East 116th Street. I was born on Hamlen Avenue, and when I was thirteen years old we moved to Dove Avenue.

I grew up in the 1990s, a time before the internet and cell phones. We had a TV, but we didn't have cable till I was well into my teens. My mom couldn't afford that. We had the radio, a record player, and a VCR for entertainment; that's it. If we wanted some other kind of stimulation, we had to come up with it ourselves. So in the summers my brother and I played outside with all the other kids that lived on our street. We also climbed the trees in our backyard, made clubhouses out of sticks and rocks, rode bikes, chased bees, patronized the ice cream man twice a day, and walked a few blocks to Drug World on Larchmere Boulevard for twenty-five-cent chips and juices. If we really felt like the hike, we could walk to Kussuth Park on Shaker Boulevard—the closest park to us. Every kid on the street went in the house the moment the streetlights came on.

It wasn't until we moved to Dove that I got to explore East 116th Street fully. However, I grew up walking the streets and meeting new friends. I was a latchkey kid, which meant that while my mom went to work right after school I looked after myself. In the mornings I had to wake up and get ready, then I had to lock the doors before I left the house, walk to the bus stop at the end of my VERY LONG street at 6:30 a.m., then after school I had to walk from Hamlen to Parkview Avenue to get to our sitter. I saw my mother really early in the mornings as we all hurried around the bathroom, really late at night after she was done for the day, and on weekends (though she'd usually just be sleeping then).

So much of my childhood was shaped by the experiences I had on East 116th. On those LONG walks to Parkview after school everyday, I would often wander the streets and therefore was picked up by the police on a regular basis. I learned every tree and landmark and sound to help me find my way around. I was rescued by my brother from two separate sexual assaults on Hamlen. I spent a lot of time looking through books I wanted to read at Rice Branch Library. I've been jumped by groups of my peers on Browning Avenue and on East 115th and Woodland Avenue. I got my hair done regularly at the beauty parlor on East 116th and Buckeye, across from the Finast shopping center. I used to stare in awe as neighbors engaged in knife fights in the streets after dark; those from Morris Black would wander onto our street, and people would come out to defend us. I attended Harvey Rice for kindergarten, then Cleveland School of the Arts from 1990 to when I graduated in 1999; fourth through twelfth grade.

My mom wasn't a cook, so East 116th Street was a paradise of food for us. Our closest food Mecca was Buckeye and East 116th, where across from Harvey Rice was Snapps and Wendy's. Down towards MLK Boulevard was McDonald's. That was our favorite place to eat. Closer to our street there was KFC off 125th and Buckeye, and Geppetto's Pizzeria on Turney Road next to Blockbuster Video, where we went twice a month on Saturday nights.

One other thing I loved about East 116th Street was how the entire street felt like one small town. Family was important when I was growing up, but so were those you lived near. There wasn't one street along East 116th where I didn't know at least one face. Everyone's kids played together; we all went to the same schools; we all rode the same school buses; we all rode the #50 bus up and down those twisty East 116th bumps and turns. We all watched the Rapids race up and down Shaker Boulevard; we all shopped at the same stores; we all ate the same foods. We had pride in each little corner of East 116th we inhabited, but we didn't gate keep others from those experiences. I like the people on Cromwell better than those on Browning; Forest residents were mysterious while Shaker Boulevard was like a second home. East 116th Street was truly my whole world.

I can talk about so many more landmarks and what they meant to me growing up. East 116th Street shaped who I am today. East 116th showed me the nostalgic, the fun, the traumatic, and the uglies of life. As attached as I am to my roots, I wanted different experiences in the world. I didn't want East 116th Street to be the only lens I saw life through. It is my fundamental; my baseline; but not my destination.

II. The Places We Remember Is the Cleveland That Is Loved

Ode to the Hungarian and African Cultures

LOLA FARRON (Buckeye-Shaker)

From Shaker Heights to Tower City,
RTA tracks are still an anchor.
back and forth upon the path
yet I still feel much rancor.

Can we folks still live together
and integrate a few?
smug and fear, mistrust, "You seem weird"
let's begin anew.

Remember lush and colorful gardens,
There was ne'er a beetle or bug.
now there's dirt and boarded window
as barriers to hard drugs.

Noisy construction has been completed,
Harvey Rice looks just great.
yet a prejudicial pandemic, lost empathy...
still greet folks at the gate.

I sense a universal spirit,
mixing arts and history,
family pride, heritage alive
differences needn't repel as mystery.

From Shaker Heights to Tower City
RTA tracks are still an anchor.
back and forth upon the path,
can we get help from our Maker?

Let the Music Play

VICTORIA DAVIS (Larchmere)

Deep breath in, deep breath out
This is what we do
We respond to life by returning to our nature
The authentic parts of us that must live
Quite literally I could walk down the street and see yogis in the grass
Reminding travelers to be kind
Festivals and parades
Farmers markets
Street sales
Art shows
It's all needed
Summer breaks and student life
Intricately beaded
Many of us recycle because we believe in protecting the divine earth
Some of us walk
But most of us run because we see when we are needed
Social justice lives here
In a place that has seen a divide
Shaker or Cleveland
Which part are you from?
And why do we ask?
We all know better but better isn't always accessible
History says we must remember our battles
Because many of them have not yet been won
So we continue to let the music play
Drummers, you hear them.
The African beats send waves of chills every time they come alive
If the instruments could talk
They might say, listen before you speak
They might say, don't act before knowing the truth
Dog walkers take a look at what's near
Families out for a stroll
And sometimes those who are hurting too
I'm glad that even when people are different

They can walk and talk and just be
That's how it should be right?
They too get to let their music play
I can only imagine the way life was
Before integration allowed for more space
Though we have far to go, we still know how to live in the present
Because presently we need one another
Nature shows us this everyday
We walk down the street into troubled waters
We turn around to get relief through the hill of the upbeat
Equity says we all need a fair hill
Traveling through and through to the shaker square
A place of wonder yet simplicity
It feels warm and it feels cold depending on the day
When the Sunday bells ring
We are reminded to pray
Let's all heal here
It's what we deserve
Black lives matter
You'll see on the windows of homes reflecting the hearts of people who want change
So although things are familiar
We know familiar is not always enough
So we keep creating
Even when the going gets tough
We let the music play
When others say stop
Because we know we need hope
And that's all we've got.

Brownie's

SHELLEY ANDREWS-HINDERS

(Detroit-Shoreway)

Who remembers Brownie's? No, not the dessert or the Girl Scout classification, nor the simple Kodak camera that brought snapshot photography to the masses. I'm not referring to Cleveland's elfin football team mascot, either. I'm talking about the little Brownie's Tavern on Herman Avenue at the southeast corner of West 54th Street, where they made the best burgers on Cleveland's west side. I have spent futile hours online searching through Cleveland historical archives of beloved restaurants and eateries and taverns. No Brownie's to be found. How sad.

When Doe and I were courting way back in the early 1980s, Brownie's was one of our favorite cheap date destinations. Doe introduced me to the Brownie burger, and, for the price, it was love at first bite.

Our actress friend, Sharron DeCosta, longtime veteran of countless musicals at Near West Theatre, vividly remembers Brownie's. Sharron has lived her entire life on Herman Avenue. I reached out to her to ask her what she might remember about the place.

"When I get to heaven my first request will be a Brownie burger!" was her swift and enthusiastic response. "I grew up there. My dad was a regular and all the kids in the neighborhood were welcome there. It was our Applebee's. My dad stopped there every night after work, so we knew, if we needed Dad between 4:00 and 4:30 that he'd be at Brownie's, with Bob, Buzzard, Bill, and all his other neighborhood friends."

"It was truly our family restaurant. My dad did a lot of Christmas shopping there because Brownie could get stuff "right off the truck." (Wink, wink, nudge, nudge.)

Sharron claims that Brownie was in a polyamorous relationship. "His wife was his wife, but Helen lived with them, and it was well known that she was more than just his barmaid."

Sharron remembers that he had candy and chips for all the neighborhood kids to buy. "It was totally normal for a seven-year-old to walk into the bar and ask for a pop. They'd open it for you if you asked." She also remembers how clean he kept the premises. "You didn't spit your gum out on HIS sidewalk," she says, "He'd come after you." She also remembers that the tavern was always filled with plenty of tchotchkes.

"Crazy statues, and those birds that tipped and seemed to drink."

But, mostly, Sharron remembers the Brownie burgers.

"Believe it or not, they cooked them with WATER! I'm serious! They were heavenly. I have never had anything like them before or since. My first meal in heaven will be a mushroom steak burger made by Brownie."

In the grand scheme of things, Brownie's was probably no big deal, just another mom-and-pop establishment that sustained a family and a neighborhood for years and then quietly vanished. But neighborhoods and families and cities are held together by our collective memories and the indelible landscapes of childhood.

With all the manic building and redevelopment going on in our neighborhoods these days, how many other Cleveland memories are being erased, even as you read this?

Today, I celebrate a memory fragment of Cleveland's past. A row of townhouses now stands where Brownie's had been. Probably none of its current occupants have any idea that a beloved tavern once stood where they now dwell. But Sharron remembers. Fondly.

Hough Avenue

BRUCE CHECEFSKY (Hough)

On a hot summer afternoon, three youngsters were selling bottles of iced water from the corner of East 55th Street and Carnegie Avenue. The taller of the two boys leaned against a metal fence that lined the sidewalk. Sun glistened off his dark skin. The runner, the kid that runs into the street with the bottles of water, was sitting on an ice chest with a fistful of dollar bills splayed in his hand like a fan. A girl with long hair sat next to him. They couldn't have been more than twelve or thirteen years old.

The boys took turns running the water bottles to cars waiting at the traffic light. A Buick LeSabre pulled up. An older man waved. "Two bottles," he shouted from inside his car, the passenger side window down. He handed two bills out the window in exchange for the water.

Thunderstorms rolled across the city late in the afternoon. Strong wind gusts twisted the tree branches of a towering oak in an empty lot across the street from my house. A flash of lighting struck a utility pole next to A to Z Furniture & Appliances store. Interior lights flickered then the store went dark. A police car raced up Hough Avenue with sirens screaming and lights flashing followed by an ambulance. As night rolled in, the cityscape disappeared in the fog.

On a walk through the neighborhood on the following morning, I stopped at East 44th Street and Cedar Avenue, the site of the former Phillis Wheatley Hotel. In 1911, Jane Edna Hunter established a settlement house for Black women relocating from the South. Mrs. Hunter led an interracial effort to form the Working Girls Association and build a boarding home for ten women at East 40th Street, north of Central Avenue. Later that year, a two-story building at 2265 East 40th Street was purchased. The building was named after Phillis Wheatley, in honor of a late eighteenth-century Boston slave considered the first African American poet. In 1927, the Phillis Wheatley Association built a new nine-story building at 4450 Cedar Avenue. The visionary project was seen as an exemplary self-help organization that permitted young girls to maintain both heritage and self-respect.

In 1936, a black postal worker named Victor Hugo Green published *The Negro Motorist Green Book,* a resource to Black people living in, and traveling through, America. *The Green Book* was a listing of restaurants, hotels, gas stations, vacation destinations, barbershops, and other businesses they could frequent without facing discrimination and threats of violence. The Phillis Wheatley Hotel was listed among the Cleveland sites. Other the Ward Hotel, Manhattan Restaurant, and State Restaurant on Cedar Avenue, and Carnegie Hotel, Geraldine Hotel, Y.M.C.A, Majestic Hotel, Mrs. Fannie Gilmer Tourist House, and Mrs. Edith Wilkins Tourist House, all located on the east side of Cleveland.

Today, the Phillis Wheatley Association provides residential, occupational, and cultural opportunities for unmarried African American working women. Programs include dance and music lessons at the Sutphen School of Music, childcare and after school programs at the Josephine Kohler Day Care Center, summer camp for children at Camp Mueller, affordable housing for low-income senior citizens, cafeteria-style meals in the refurbished dining room, social activities and special events for the community.

I continued my walk across East 44th Street to Chester Avenue then headed east back towards the Hough neighborhood in the late afternoon. When I got to East 66th Street, I cut north to Hough Avenue where I pondered at the beauty of Château Hough, a unique vineyard and winery located in the neighborhood. Mansfield Frazier founded the Vineyard of Château Hough in 2010. The Château produces fine wines and also serves as a halfway house, which employs ex-convicts through landscaping and vineyard work.

Frazier, in a recent article for *The Observer*, said, "If I were to say Chateau Hunting Valley, people would say 'well of course.' If I were to say, Chateau Westlake, where there are a lot of wealthy gated communities, people would say 'well naturally.' When you say Chateau Hough, people think of the black community and say, 'where are you getting Chateau Hough from?' I'm saying that the land we occupy in Hough is as valuable to us as their land is to them."

Château Hough produces wines from seven Ohio-grown varieties, including the red Frontenac and white Traminette grape. Frontenac wines are rich in aromas of peach and apricot with hints of enticing citrus and tropical fruit. Traminette exudes spicy and floral aromas, alongside flavors of apricot and honey. These white wines pairs well with roasted meats and Portobello mushrooms and tend to compliment spicy flavors like Cajun shrimp.

With a bottle of Flame Dry Red Wine snuggly tucked under my arm for later, I continued three blocks north to Lexington Avenue and the League Park baseball park. Built in 1891 as a wood structure and rebuilt with concrete and steel in 1910, League Park was home to the Cleveland Spiders of the National League from 1891 to 1899. Left fielder Jesse Burkett and pitcher Cy Young, both National Baseball Hall of Fame inductees, played for the Spiders during the seven straight winning seasons under manager Patsy Tebeau.

In the late 1940s, the park was the home field of the Cleveland Buckeyes of the Negro American League. League Park was rededicated in 2014 as the Baseball Heritage Museum and Fannie Lewis Community Park at League Park.

Fixing my sights on getting home, I hiked up Lexington Avenue to East 79th Street then turned right past the empty lot at the intersection of Hough Avenue where the Seventy-Niner's Café once stood. The white-owned bar was popular with African American residents of the community in the 1960s. While details remain unclear, one of the bar owners denied water to an African American man who had entered the bar sometime on the night of July 18, 1966, and then posted a racially derogatory sign on the door. A crowd of angry African Americans gathered around the bar. People began throwing rocks at the windows and tried to set fire to the building. Later that evening, about 200 rioters roamed over a thirty-square block area centered on Hough Avenue looting stores and setting fires to business establishments.

When Cleveland Police arrived, the crowd threw rocks at them. More than 300 police officers finally showed up forcing a showdown between police force and rioters. A twenty-six-year-old African American mother of three was shot in the head, and Alton Burks was shot in the hip. Wallace Kelly was shot in the jaw.

By July 19, 1966, Cleveland City Council members John W. Kellogg and Edward F. Katalinas pressured Cleveland Mayor Locher and Police Chief Richard Wagner to call in the Ohio Army National Guard. Governor Rhodes declared a state of emergency in Cleveland and deployed 1,500 National Guardsmen to the Hough neighborhood. Rioting spread resulting in more bottle and rock throwing and looting. The damage was extensive.

Cleveland Police shot a mother, three of her young children, and her teenaged nephew near East 107th Street and Cedar Avenue the following night. Cleveland City Councilman M. Morris Jackson, who represented Hough, pressed the mayor to declare martial law. Mayor Locher refused and declined to impose a curfew. Major General Erwin C. Hostetler,

Adjutant General of the Ohio Army National Guard, issued an order authorizing his troops to shoot looters and arsonists. African American Benoris Toney was shot in the head in the parking lot of the Dougherty Lumber Co.

The total number killed in the riots was four; over fifty sustained serious injuries. Racism and poverty were the main cause of the upsizing, according to some. Others suggested that Black nationalists or communists had caused the Hough Riots. City of Cleveland elected officials claimed that the riot had been planned by violent, Black nationalist or communist organizations. *The Plain Dealer* supported their unsubstantiated claims in a front-page article.

A year later, Carl Stokes became the first African American mayor of a major US city when he was elected mayor of Cleveland.

Boarding the #38 RTA bus along Hough Avenue past the Hough Food Deal Market where customers can buy beverages and lottery tickets, food and home supplies, human hair, wigs, and hair accessories, I glance out the window at Invigorate Gallery at East 68th Street, where artists from the Hough neighborhood had panels mounted to the facade of the building that read, "I survived the Hough Riots," "Growing your own food is like printing your own money," and "If you even dream of beating me you'd better wake up . . . and apologize."

Near East 55th Street, I saw two men on a scissors lift working to restore a colorful 150-foot long mural on the side of the Fannie M. Lewis Community Corrections and Treatment Center. The mural, first completed in 2000 by Cleveland artist Mark Howard, is a dazzling arrangement of figures climbing ladders, waving out from windows, and general gestures of friendship and hope. Howard, born in Newark, NJ, has been painting and selling religious pictures since he was ten years old. "I used to paint scenes on clam shells when we were down in Nantucket during summers," he was quoted saying in a local newspaper recently. "Picket Fences," at the Hopkins International Airport Continental Airlines underground walkway, is his most widely known work.

I stepped off the bus with my bottle of Flame Dry Red Wine still unopened. Night was setting in. Rain clouds had lifted giving the evening a cool sparking shine.

When I returned home, I watched the local news. Federal agents had reportedly moved into Cleveland to protect the Anthony J. Celebrezze Federal Building following the recent Black Lives Matter protests. Mayor Jackson and Police Chief Williams tried to squash the rumors claiming the agents were sent by the Justice Department as criminal investigators, not federal troops.

I filled my wine glass and muted the television. "We've heard that before," I muttered to myself.

A Tour of Lake View Cemetery

KARIM RAGAB (Little Italy)

Prelude.
Every morning in the summertime I take a long walk around Lake View Cemetery. Lake View is an old garden cemetery, established from 1868–1870 by a group of Cleveland businessmen, including Jeptha Wade, Henry B. Payne, and Joseph Perkins. The first plots were in use by October 1870. Over 100,000 people are buried in the bounds of Lake View. Over 100,000 stories reached their final end there. Some famous people associated with Cleveland are buried in the cemetery, including John Rockefeller, James A. Garfield, Eliot Ness, Harvey Pekar, and Alan Freed. There are also tens of thousands of names carved on tombstones in the cemetery that have been long forgotten by history. It is a beautiful place, a garden, a reprieve from the busy city. I wake with the sun and make a cup of coffee. I put on my shoes, smoke a cigarette on the porch of my apartment on Coltman and walk five minutes to the Euclid gate. Then, taking a deep breath, I enter the cemetery for a long stroll.

I.
Death haunts my steps
Like the shadow of my body
The sun casts onto the road.
I can still feel the burn of
The cigarette on the back
Of my throat.
What is death?
The end of our stories.
The end of everything,
Or perhaps a new beginning
In an undiscovered country
Whose bounty we can only
Imagine.
I pass grave after grave,
Marble crosses,
Jewish stars,
A statue of a buck, a statue of a horse,

And nowhere do I find consolation from
Death.
I am surrounded by death
But also by life
Because Lake View is a garden cemetery.
In the summertime
Everything blossoms and blooms.
I know that in the autumn,
Nothing will last,
Just like our lives
These green leaves
Will flame out
And turn to brown ash
Littering the graves.

II.
Once I told my ex
That I loved her here,
Sitting on the edge,
Near the dam.
I told her that I loved her
And she told me the same.
We've separated since then.
The love never died in my heart.
Perhaps that's the thing about love:
It is the one thing
That even death cannot touch,
Which death,
Or separation
Only serves to deepen
In a way
That wrenches the heart
From the cage
Of bone
Surrounding it.

III.
I sobbed here,
In the cemetery,

By the lake,
When I received a phone call
In which my dad
Told me
That my stepmother had breast cancer.
It was a dark day, I remember.
The whole sky was smothered
By oppressive clouds.
My stepmother has since recovered.
Her cancer was only stage 1.
Still,
I cannot think of her now,
Without thinking of
The shadow of death
That hangs over us all.

IV.
I lived a full life.
I've burned like the sun.
I've screamed at the stars.
I've been drunk and high beneath the
Velvet vault of heaven.
I've fallen in love
And had my heart broken
Time and time again.
I've kissed in cars
And downtown bars.
I've felt the summer's scalding heat
And the winter's bitter chill.
There's nothing left to do,
Yet time future and time past,
Are perhaps contained in time present,
So as I walk
I know that my whole story is contained
In each and every step.
Down the cemetery's nature trail
There is a crossroads.
To the left the path is straight and sun-strewn
Today.

To the right the path turns into the shaded wood.
And I picked my path,
Just as I picked my life,
Wondering
If I made the choice at all.

V.
I leave the silence of the cemetery
At the Mayfield gate
And walk down the steep hill
Into the city,
Little Italy,
Where people even in a pandemic
Are gathered
Eating fresh pizza and cannolis,
While Bob Seeger
Plays from "La Dolce Vita" bar.
Here is the absence of death.
Here is life in the city: vibrant, present, full.
Memories of death
(The shadow)
Flee like night at daybreak.
I sit at Presti's,
Order a slice of pie
And try to forget all that I know
In order that I might live
Again.

Glenville: The Transformation of a Community into a Neighborhood

CAROLYN COOPER (Glenville)

Google's Online Dictionary describes a COMMUNITY as being:

1. A group of people living in the same place or having a particular characteristic in common.
2. A feeling of fellowship with others, as a result of sharing common attitudes, interests, and goals.

And it describes a NEIGHBORHOOD as simply being:

1. The area surrounding a particular place, person, or object.

Growing up in the Glenville community was an awesome experience for me, because I felt completely safe in my ward. And I can recall so many beautiful childhood memories.

I had such a wonderful, loving family! I grew up the youngest and the only female amongst two older siblings in a two-parent, middle-class household. Also, I loved my best friend's large nine-member family, who all lived in the house next door to me for many years.

Additionally, I'm very proud that I received a stellar education in the Cleveland public school system. Through my elementary school's French Club, I was able to study abroad in France (at the tender age of eleven years old) and celebrate my twelfth birthday in that beautiful country.

During my school years, I loved how all of the parents in the community always supported each other, supported the neighborhood children, helped our teachers, and our principal.

Our mothers were the unsalaried lunch ladies, the paraprofessionals, the assistant librarians, and the school secretaries.

Plus, our dads attended weekly fathers' club meetings, attended our school events, and accompanied us on field trips. Parents were practically the school staff and were always willing to help out.

I can remember after working a night nursing shift, my mom would stay up to fry chicken and make side dishes. Then she would brown bag the food to provide individual lunches for my entire class, my teacher, and the other parent chaperones attending the field trip.

Another classmate's mom would bake cakes, slice them, and individually wrap them to add to our lunches. Yet another would pack bags of ice, bottled water, juice boxes, paper napkins, paper plates, and utensils to contribute to our class.

No one ever asked the parents to do this or reimbursed any of them. They always volunteered and donated whatever they could, because we were one big extended family.

Furthermore, when someone passed away in the community, everyone comforted the grieving family and expressed sympathy for their loss.

Meals were delivered to their homes, cards containing monetary gifts were placed in their hands, flowers were ordered and delivered to the funeral home, and the neighborhood shed tears with them at the "homegoing" service.

Flash-forward to this present day. The once pleasant, giving, caring, well-manicured Glenville community has transformed into a neighborhood filled with crime, trash, jealously, hate, drug abuse, gunshots, many vacant houses, a lot of run down streets, and multiple grassy lots.

Gone are the majority of parents and grandparents who were once the cornerstones of this community. They have all transitioned into our ancestors—bequeathing property to their children and grandchildren.

However, most of their bloodlines failed to carry out the community values of the past. Many of their historic houses fell into foreclosure and are now condemned or were demolished due to unpaid property taxes.

Gone are most of the children and grandchildren from this neighborhood. They left and are now raising their families elsewhere.

If Glenville could talk, it would tell all of its listeners how great it once was, and how living in a community is far greater than just surviving in a neighborhood.

The Old Neighborhood

JO DONOFRIO (Detroit-Shoreway)

I used to love to listen to my dad's stories about what he fondly called "the old neighborhood." Those were the days; when he was a boy and when neighborhoods were all about being neighborly. Everyone knew each other, took pride in their neighborhood and felt like they belonged. They worked hard, supported each other and were willing to sacrifice to achieve their dreams.

My grandparents were Italian immigrants who came to the United States in the early 1900s in search of a better life. They settled in the Near West Side of Cleveland, near West 67th and Detroit, in the area now known as Gordon Square. It was one of four areas in Greater Cleveland where large numbers of Italian immigrants settled to find a job, buy a house, and raise a family.

As a child, I spent a lot of time in the old neighborhood visiting my grandfather. From riding through the Baltic tunnel as my dad honked the horn, picking tomatoes in my grandfather's garden, and always asking "What time is it?" as we drove by the clock tower at the Cudell Center. And then there were the annual trips to Edgewater Park for the Fourth of July fireworks and to Our Lady of Mt. Carmel's annual festival.

The church, which was originally located at 7200 Detroit Road where the Craciun Berry Funeral Home is now, served as the cornerstone of the community for many years. My dad, who was one of the original altar boys, often told us the story of how he and the other boys would go every Saturday with Father Vincent to collect bricks to build the new church which still stands on the corner of West 70th and Detroit.

My brother, sister and I looked forward to the annual Our Lady of Mt. Carmel Festival every July and the Sunday procession through the streets, which continues even today. My dad seemed to know everyone at the festival and afterwards, of course, had many more stories to tell. The annual festival which began in 1926, one year after my father was born, was canceled in 2020 for the first time in more than ninety years, due to the pandemic.

In his elder years, I would occasionally take my dad down to the old neighborhood. He would take such pride in pointing out where he and my mother had their wedding reception in 1946, on the second floor of the building on West 67th and Detroit where the LGBT Community Center of Greater Cleveland is now located. He also always showed me one more time the house where he grew up on West 67th or where Isabella Brother's Bakery used to be on West 69th.

As residents started to migrate to the suburbs, it was sad to watch the old neighborhood deteriorate. Though the building of the Gordon Square Arts District has brought new life to the area, it has also changed it. While much has been gained, much has been lost. Due to gentrification, the influx of businesses and less affordable housing, it became difficult for many longtime residents to remain in the area.

I often wonder what my dad would think of "the old neighborhood" now. How amazed he would be at the redevelopment, the increase in housing values and the influx of young couples and families. What would he think of the high-priced condos at Battery Park, the same area where he used to play baseball down by the railroad tracks? And the reopening of the Capitol Theatre where, as a child, it cost him twenty-five cents to go to a matinee.

Still today, signs of the once proud and prospering Italian neighborhood remain. You don't have to look far to find telephone poles, benches, and fire hydrants still painted red, white, and green or streets named after priests who once served at the church. Each time I visit Gordon Square, I can still hear my dad's voice and his stories about a different place in different time. It many ways, for me, it will always be "the old neighborhood."

Lee-Harvard Happiness

LESILIE PRICE (Lee-Harvard)

I had never played in the street before. Just the idea of it made me giddy, but despite the two boys who lived next door, throwing a football over my eight-year-old head as I stood on the sidewalk, Mom forbade my participation. I was an obedient child, her only daughter who preferred Barbie over books, knew how to climb a tree and when to have my feet planted in the front yard before it got dark. Our house was almost dead center in the block; the one with the steepest sloped driveway, perfect for riding my skateboard seated so I could turn just in time to land on the soft tree-lawn grass.

We were the first family to integrate Biltmore Avenue, or so we thought, but within two years of our making our arrival in the Lee-Harvard area, the rest of the neighborhood resembled my family; a mom, a dad and more children to play with me. I made fast friends with both sides of the neighbor's children, each had at least another young girl for me to play with; kickball or dolls in the back yard under the shade of overgrown trees and the watchful eye of either set of parents, since no fencing had been erected yet and gardens consisted of only flowering bushes adding color to backyards with plenty of grass that always needed cutting. Thank goodness I was not interested in boys (yet), so Mom would let me go with either neighbor's son who showed up at the side door asking politely if I was available to play, requesting the accompaniment of my skateboard just in case.

My grade school was located across Lee Road, just under three blocks down my street, which made walking to school easy in my mind, but my father insisted that I ride in the car those three blocks, only picking up the neighborhood children we knew well, waving to those I knew I would only see again later in the hallway at Gracemount. Not until I reached teenager status and Dad's recurring shift change at the post office did I learn what I had missed all those years; the chance to spend my allowance on penny candy and bubble gum and discovering the vast collection of cigarettes to choose from in a time I was sent to purchase whatever I wanted as long as I brought home a pack of Pall Malls for my mom. For a long time, the school's yard was as far as I could go, but it sat just across the street from my childhood babysitter, Mrs. Hunter, whose family consisted of more children I could count, learning later who actually lived there, and those like me who were picked up at the end of the day so their parents could work. Mrs. Hunter had more toys than I had ever seen along with a double swing and a sliding board in her back yard. For eight years it was my home away from home, steps away from school, where I learned I liked Yoo-hoo chocolate drink, burnt grilled cheese sandwiches, and making the legs of the swing set slide out of the ground if I pumped my legs hard enough to make it go higher.

I always felt safe as I ventured throughout the three blocks to the south to Mrs. Hunter's house and school. It was easy to get almost anything we wanted from Gardell's on the corner, but back then wanting for anything more than a new drawing pad and crayons was rare. I purchased my first can of tennis balls about five years later outgrowing the candy treats forbidden by my new set of braces, learning to "play" with an old discarded racquet, hitting balls against the school's brick wall imagining what a real tennis court would like. Gracemount only had basketball courts at the time and once school was let out, the older neighborhood boys filled them with laughter.

When I was not on my skateboard, I was on my bicycle navigating the sidewalk that separated the neatly cut grass from the stately grown trees. Everyone's house was beautiful, neat, and well kept. Rarely was there a parked car anywhere but in the neighbor's driveways, leaving the streets open for an occasional game of flag football or tag against the children across the street. At eight years old, life was uncomplicated and filled with fun. Every summer evening, we caught fireflies and filled at least two glass jars that Dad would punch holes into the lid to let the air in, just small enough to keep the trapped bugs from flying out.

On hot summer days, Mom would lay a blanket in the back yard under the large oak tree so we could sit outside after the sun set, letting the warm air and the cool grass cradle us to sleep. Of course, this only happened on Friday nights when work was on hold for the weekend and Dad had the late shift at the Post Office. As the noise of the neighborhood died down, you could hear the buzz of someone's television in the background, muffled sounds discussing the day's news until the crickets won your ear's attention. It was not until the next day that we learned about the boy who got a liver from a monkey with Dad mentioning it was the strangest thing he had ever heard, especially with a war going on. I thought so too.

The war seemed so far away compared to the peaceful nature of Biltmore Avenue. Only two weeks prior Mom celebrated her thirty-eighth birthday in the back yard under that oak tree. Dad finished the brick patio the previous year and built a table out of an old pole and a door in form of a contraption that was assembled only for their backyard entertaining. Mom and I set up colorful folding chairs haphazardly around the yard while Dad flamed the charcoal fire in the grill, summoning the neighbors and their lifelong friends to the backyard. Dad had been a photojournalist at a local paper, the Call & Post, before working at the post office, a change he told Mom he had to make because the paper just didn't pay enough for the new house, braces, and the new Cutlass Mom wanted. That day the grownups filled my summer slumber spot with hot dogs and tall glasses, ice ringing as they drank and cigarette smoke curling up to the branches as they laughed. On weekend party days, I was only allowed to go to the Winston's back yard, just far enough that both sets of parents could keep an eye on the four of us from a yard away, forbidden from going inside incase mischief ensued with my playmates' little brother.

I knew we were not poor. Dad said he grew up poor and owning a home made him anything but. I knew I was black. Back then Dad said we were Negroes and for some reason I sensed there was something special about the color of my skin. Not only was it a big deal that everyone around me on Biltmore Avenue was a Negro, but we were doing something good for the world, coming together and moving into neighborhood we had never lived before, despite the fact that no sooner than we had moved in, we never got to know the white neighbors before they moved somewhere else. It was alright with me because I got playmates that looked like me and wanted to be around me, unlike the people that only stayed in their homes shortly after we moved in. That was no fun from what I remember.

July was hot in Cleveland with days filled with sprinkler parties and balloon fights, bicycle rides to the corner and push up ice pops if you stayed out of trouble. Dad let me use an old camera albeit without film, to practice taking pictures in preparation for my future Girl Scout badge, but at the time my membership in the Brownies was on hold for the summer and I could only practice when he was awake to watch me do it just right. Dad's late-night shift had him eating dinner before heading off to work during most days of the week. He read the newspaper every day and talked to Mom about the plight of the Negro, feeling agitated with everything that was going on across the nation and ultimately in our own "back yard."

I had only been back to my neighborhood a month that July, after spending time with my grandparents on their farm in Oberlin, Ohio.

There my community consisted of pigs, cows, three dogs, two stray cats that belonged to the landowners behind us, and a chicken coop with baby chicks. As much as I loved the farm, I missed watching the next-door neighbors' children chase whatever newfound ball they took from another's yard and playing board games with my new best friend who lived two houses down. Mom let me venture down an extra house once Sherri and I discovered each other's love of Trouble and Life. Sherri's mom and my mom starting meeting for lunch on occasion at the Arthur Treacher's on Lee Road when the men of the house were home. Local restaurants were where the grownups went to "treat themselves," not a place for children my parents would insist. I had just finished beating Sherri in our second game of Trouble when Mom said I had to come home. Now.

It was a Tuesday evening and Dad had been awake for over an hour, but instead of reading the *Plain Dealer* at the kitchen table, both he and Mom were glued to the television set with its multiple shades of gray images moving loudly across the screen. I recognized the quick flash of an image of Martin Luther King, but the rest was a blur. Dad said racial tension had reached its peak across America and had arrived in Cleveland. I remember thinking that I did not know what racial tension looked like but was afraid that it had arrived where I lived because it had both my parents on edge like I had never seen before.

For the rest of the week, I was not allowed to leave the yard and my days with Mrs. Hunter waiting for Mom to come home from work came to an end. Now my cousin Patty was my new playmate, someone who I rarely saw except for family events to the "other side of town." I remembered that she was my babysitter on occasion in the third-floor bedroom when the adults played cards at her parent's house. She had books and no board games, saying she had outgrown them years ago. I was half her age, but she attended a school called Glenville. I wondered if all schools started with G. Since it was the summer, she arrived with only her clothes, no books, hastily jammed in square, brown leather suitcase that had been made worse for wear. It was like I had a sister, but I was not sure I liked the idea since she appeared out of nowhere. She was older than all my friends, even the sister of my friend across the street who had been sent to reform school last year was younger and not interested in making her acquaintance in the summer heat. I was told to mind Patty during the day and to keep the noise outside and to a minimum because Dad slept during the day. Luckily, he slept in the cool basement, comforted by the low hum of the dehumidifier. There was nothing in the basement for me or Patty, so we had no reason to disturb him. It would be another ten years before the basement was transformed to the family room with a console television and a stereo inside.

The back yard was preferred by the adults and shaded by the oak tree, but we preferred to play in the front yard in the blazing sun, rolling down the hill, letting the grass cool our faces before landing next to the sidewalk which for the week was the battleground line that we were not allowed to cross. Getting close was exciting. If Vaniece was home next door we would play dolls in her driveway if I sat on the edge of my grass. Patty would perch on the front stoop with a watchful eye because dolls were for kids. The view was perfection. Our driveway was the highest and steepest on the block, allowing you to see all the way to the cross street about ten houses down in both directions. As long as no car was parked in the driveway before the houses, sometimes I could see traffic on Lee Road, but the lighting had to be exactly right and my imagination on overdrive.

On Wednesday, some of the neighbors gathered on the sidewalk, just the adults since most of the children were told to stay in the yard. Sherri's baby sister was latched to her father's leg, so I pretended that she was the spy to report back to the rest of us who looked on but had no clue to their discussions. Mom found me in the driveway sitting on my skateboard, announcing that dinner was ready. Patty ascended from the basement as I entered the side door of our colonial. Twelve steps to the right went down, and three steps to the right went up, but Mom must have sent her down there for a reason. It was never a place I freely wanted to go. Dad stepped in a few minutes behind me, clutching his edition of the *Plain Dealer* in his hand. "There's a race riot in Hough. Unrest might spill out into other neighborhoods, let us just hope ours is not one of them." Dad opened his newspaper as we gathered around the kitchen table, nestled safely inside, but the headlines confirmed his announcement.

By the end of the week of July 16, 1966, I felt vulnerable in my neighborhood for the first time. Play time was limited and although I loved my house and especially my yard, I missed walking about freely especially to Sherri's house. Mom and Dad both had strict rules that week, but they lasted for the rest of the month. Patty stayed with us for almost two weeks, but her parents picked her up on a Saturday and drove her to Oberlin to stay with an aunt. I was not allowed to go. Mom said she preferred that I stay where she could see me. By the end of the week and despite the eighty degree heat, my friends were relegated to their back yards or trapped inside, instilled with fear about events beyond our neighborhood, afraid those riots would find us behind the tree lawn strips since the street was no longer a safe place to be.

Everyone's fears were confirmed I was told, but I never saw a riot on Biltmore Avenue. Dad said the National Guard was in town to keep the peace, so I guess their purpose had been fulfilled. There were more riots on the television, somewhere else Mom said, but things would be different in Cleveland very soon. Mom had a friend named Carl (I think it was), and she was excited about some things he talked to her about doing again. In the meantime, we had to play safe and stay in the yard in the neighborhood I loved. As things quieted around town, slowly my friends reappeared in the streets, but I discovered the front stoop to eventually be my favorite of all. Dad took away my skateboard to be on the safe side, he said, and the oversized bushes in front of the stair railing provided shade and cover when Barbie, Ken, and I wanted to be alone. Mom knew where to find me when dinner was ready. I missed seeing Sherri but going two houses down was too far during the riots, despite there being nothing but peace permeating the avenue, same birds during the day and the relentless fireflies at night. Just as I heard Mom's voice through the screen door calling for Dad that dinner was ready, I turned to look inside as her voice billowed above me. "Charles, look out the front window! Look now or you'll miss it." She stepped out onto the porch and placed both hands on my shoulder. With a calm voice and a gentle squeeze, she said to me, "Time to eat, Ladybug." I stood up as I heard my father's voice behind her, "Well I'll be damned." The three of us stood on the stoop, watching an armored vehicle, like something from the war movies Dad would watch, slowly gliding down Biltmore Avenue toward Lee Road, ensuring that there was peace in our neighborhood.

Of all the memorable events that occurred in my neighborhood, from new friends to prom photos, backyard birthday parties to losing touch with those that brought so much joy to my childhood, that single tank was galvanized as a pivotal moment of the area I called home. It reminds me today how the neighborhood and the world is connected in ways we may never actually visit but are intertwined just the same.

III. Cleveland Is For Us All

You, Me, and Us

SUJATA LAKHE (Ohio City)

A lean figure in a schoolboy haircut approached us from behind. We were in the parking lot of the iconic Cleveland landmark—the West Side Market. I, my six-year-old daughter Samira, and her friend Shaylin had our hands full of green veggies, pickling cucumbers, sweet peas in the pod, strawberries, corn, one honeydew, and one giant watermelon. One would have thought we were getting ready for some summer cookout, but no—this was my weekly visit to the historic Ohio City neighborhood, which I had been doing religiously for quite a few years now. Even when pregnant, even in bone-chilling Cleveland winter, and even before my daughter was born. Saturday morning meant driving over Hope Memorial Bridge with Cleveland downtown on the right and the smokestacks of the steel plant somewhere in the valley to the left. Taking a right turn into the parking lot of the market house, bustling with people under its Byzantine vaulted roof. A reverse L-shaped outdoor produce section cradled the building with a looming clock tower built with yellow bricks.

The lean figure said, “Hello ladies. I can help lighten some of that. Let me help you take your goodies to the car.” Sweat glistening on his pale forehead.

Samira shot a look my way with question marks for eyes. Shaylin’s wild red head whipped around silently asking me, “What’s up with this?. Usually it would be someone with pamphlets, trying to make us believe in something, collecting donations for the homeless or a community newsletter.

I had multiple plastic bags hooked on my fingers, which left thick welts as I handed a few bags to him.

The parking lot was full with cars parked in every inch available. A row of drivers lined up with eyes peeled for a spot to open. Families with skipping toddlers and squealing strollers and worried grandma’s moving in a disarray. Some with their hands full like us while others rolling their shopping bag on a two-wheel upright dolly. The parking lot had potholes, but there was no feeding the meter.

I opened the trunk on my black Honda CR-V, and the man helped us put bags in the car. I extended my hand to shake his and said, “ Girls, say hi to Congressman Kucinich. You know he is also vegetarian, just like me.”

Dennis bowed slightly to get to their eye level, "Hello young lady, what is your name?"

He proceeded with some such small talk, then he pulled out his wallet from his pocket. He opened it like a book and pulled out a laminated old photograph. It was a picture of a football team. Big guys kneeling in the front, tall guys standing in the back, and in the middle was a seated players row, among them there was one who looked extra small. Dennis pointed at that small figure with a friendly smile and said, "You see that? It's me. You know what allows me to play in the same team with these big guys"? He paused for effect. "It is my courage! Remember that."

My girls do remember this but only vaguely. However, I have held onto this moment for about fifteen years. Moments like this made me feel welcome in America, a new immigrant from India who found Cleveland's promise of cutting-edge science irresistible.

I grew up in a steel town of Bhilai Nagar, in India. A Gulmohar tree-lined boulevard connected the town's two ends. Smokestacks with the dusty coke oven and melting shop and rolling mills sprawled on one end linearly connected to the main hospital on the other. In between lived workers and officers in spartan cement "quarters" (homes) surrounded by lush gardens of roses, hyacinths, bougainvillea, jasmine, mango, guava, neem, tamarind, Jamun and Behr trees.

People loved living and working here so much that a common joke the steelworkers told was, "The only exit from Bhilai Steel Plant (BSP), was on the other end of the Central Boulevard—the circular cement tower of the hospital. That is when one died!"

This was the town where moon followed our car as Mom and Dad in the front and me and my brother in the backseat would often go Bhaaji shopping to the farmer's market on the outskirts of the town. Little did I know at the time that some of these vendors probably were displaced because their land was taken by Steel Authority of India, never realizing at the time that my family now lived in the place from where they were driven out from.

Suddenly my dad would say "close your eyes," and I would obediently close them shut.

"Now open them!" and "Look where the moon is!"

With a gasp I would realize that the moon out the right window was all of a sudden to the left. This routine never got old for him. We would be at the Saturday pop-up vegetable market, a cacophony of languages, vendors lifting up medieval-looking iron weighing scale, the kind we only see on justice statues nowadays putting weights on one pan and the vegetable of the customer's choice on the other side of the balance until the pointer hovered in the middle.

Everything newly built and organized conveniently for steelworkers, Bhilai was a mini-India as people from all over India, every language, every religion had moved into town to live side by side, when the steel plant was built seven years after India's independence. There was also a separate sector for the community of engineers and their families from what was then the country of USSR. The Soviets were there to train the newbie Indian engineers like my father to build their own steel plant. In the market, they would point to what they wanted while pushing rosy-cheeked babies in umbrella strollers. Which brings me to feeling welcome in Cleveland by the orange flames spewing from the smokestacks. The sampling of the world's people these smokestacks brought to Cleveland and who eventually called Cleveland their home. The cacophony of Spanish, German, East Asian, Eastern European, and some Indian languages overheared when shopping at West Side Market. Seeing Babushka's with triangular scarfs tied under their chin refreshing my childhood memory of a gift of Matrushka doll. Fragrant oriental lily advertising for the corner flower shop, cumin and paneer-like cheese sold in the Greek store and bargaining! All stimulating that part of my brain which remained unstirred in rest of America.

New beginning, new girlhood, the same moon followed me on I-90 as I went looking for familiarity in Cleveland, once called the Forest City. Tree-lined streets emanating from downtown and radiating towards suburbs. When I arrived in Cleveland on a snowy January evening in 1990, remnants of steel industry from over hundred years ago, including iron ore carrier, William G. Mather, anchored in the lake, dotted the city. If you stood on the top floor of Tower City in downtown you could see the smokestacks of the still functioning steel mills to the south. To the far east one could see the Cleveland Clinic, the location of my first job. While early Cleveland blacksmiths worked iron, it was 1857 when the industry really got rolling, predating Bhilai Steel by almost a century. Spanakopita replaced Samosa. Falafel replaced Bhujia. Vegetable run with my daughter replaced vegetable run with my mom and grandma. Watching crepes being made from the second floor mezzanine of the West Side Market replaced watching dosa being made from the second floor of the Mumbai railway station. Banana-Nutella or whatever you wanted to put on the French crepes, even spinach or feta-crepes made fresh to the order on the spot. Although sometimes the chef dished out not so sweet a treat. Once he yelled at a man who was taking a video.

"Idiot, get out of here! Why you filming me?" Addressing the crowd, "These tourists, they don't want to buy anything, and they are in the way of my customers." To this day I cannot figure out what was that all was about.

I recently asked my daughter, who is starting senior year of computer sciences at Cornell this fall, "Do you remember about going to the West Side Market with me?"

"Yeah," her face filling up my phone. "Fish smell and the whole pig in the case and the vegetable market."

"What about vegetable market?"

"You know, the vibes. How so many people knew you."

Several years later, on an August 2020 afternoon when I was visiting in the midst of the pandemic year, the second floor mezzanine was vacant. No eating out of paper boats and watching the meat bazaar below. Crepes were still being made but in a modern looking coffee shop. Nevertheless, I still got a quick advice on how to cook the handpicked morels. I was surprised to see a heap for sale, usually morels are available only between March and May, but this year is truly bizarre—even the May apples fruited in late July! The number of produce stalls have contracted to almost half. The market appears to be drowning in bars, breweries, apartment buildings, and parking meters. No pedestrian traffic; I didn't see the familiar sight of colorful flowers arranged in white buckets in the usual place. But this was not just the COVID-19 pandemic effect. According to Vince Bertonasch, owner of now closed Vince Meats, the market never rebounded from the nine-month-long parking lot reconstruction in 2016.

To step in the building itself felt like a step in the past. Enchiladas, pierogis, Pad Thai, spanakopita, stuffed grape leaves: lots of yummy discoveries once made long ago by this vegetarian girl who blew up a pressure cooker while trying to make dhaal and put on forty pounds in her first year of living in Cleveland. However, Maha's, where I would pick up bulk falafel was gone. After thirty years in the market, owner Michael Tryczyk told the *Plain Dealer* that it was because of the plumbing and electrical issues.

I asked the lady at the sausage stand if she had any CHAE-vap-ee-chi. My Serbian coworker would bring it to grill at our summer cookouts. Even though I have never tasted it, my husband swears by its caseless explosive smoky flavor. In addition, it goes perfectly with chapatis and sautéed onions.

She made a frowny face and said, "Sorry, the previous owners did not sell us the recipe", another casualty of the time. It was sad to hear that as stalls here have remained under individual family control for much of the life of the market, several dating over a hundred years.

Once again, I was driving home over the river with a trunk full of goodies. The view of the river from the Hope Memorial Bridge was making it abundantly clear why the Native Americans would name the river Cuyahoga, meandering like my thoughts. This drive always feels more like a gliding through time to me. Cleveland downtown to the left and steel mills in the valley below on the right. Massive "Guardians of the Transportation" sculptures. Peregrine falcon nesting under the bridge where a lower deck was planned but never built. It is hard to believe that in the '70s county engineers had threatened to remove the sculptures. It is also hard to believe Dennis Kucinich was erased out of local politics by gerrymandering.

Kucinich, referred to as Ohio's oddball for proposing a Department of Peace, represented the scientific industry, which had largely replaced the steel and other manufacturing industry as the largest employer in Greater Cleveland.

Due to social distancing required to curb the spread of SARS-CoV-2, we have been cooking at home a lot again. West Side Market showing the same ingenuity of using the recycled cardboard boxes for displaying the price for each heap of healthy goodness. Foreign accented multi-generational shop owners, men and women, behind their masks, arranging and replenishing the display basket.

"Forr YOOO, I will throw in an exthrra..." the sweet man put a strong emphasis on YOU while putting extra bunch of celery in a bag for me. His "YOOO" said with rising and falling inflection. A "you" said in such a way that it meant you are part of us. That somehow validated me. It validated me more than getting my name on the first publication in a peer reviewed scientific journal.

The American dream is not about making millions or having dozens of publications or owning a large house in a leafy suburb. The American dream is turning from "you" to "us". There is a little software inside us humans which has learned over thousands of years on Earth that people similar looking to the self are not weird, are trustworthy, and, therefore, they are "us". We need to retrain that software—and retrain it fast—in this fast-moving world. Someone, even a stranger, can be part of "us" simply due to their physical proximity to us and our common interest in this world.

Neighborhood Views

FATIMAH ABOUELSOUD (Larchmere)

The reminiscing of a lover leads a deep heart out to the porch.

Light rain drops and freckles a mind that wanders higher in the sky with each breath, in and out. The eyes wander over the shells of trees that hold witness to the reconfiguring of pain. Wisdom is shared through the whispers of the leaves. Solace is found in the council of five, each singing a different chord of the season.

Here, underneath an unobstructed gaze of the universe, she looks and listens at the goings of life. Here, dogs bark at the top of a hill that overlooks a quiet, underdog city that holds so much beauty once one is willing to accept the pain. It can be a sad city, tucked under the lull of gray clouds and cold.

The air always leaves its residents tired.

Somewhere, along the edges of this grayness, pockets of color and creativity blossom from that pain. Rainbows from the refraction of art paint one's own pain in color. Under that gray sky, reflecting on self and society helps to part the clouds on any day.

The sound of a radio debate cuts through the trance, bringing her back to the rows of two-family homes. Her thoughts spark tear ducts. The fullness of her heart returns the thoughts to her trees. Elected strangers that created friendships that formed family. People who she can't imagine her life without.

She looks inside at the heat pressing up on the cooler glass, leaving drops where their cheeks touch. Inside, the air carries the enveloping scent of spice and earth, sunflower and coconut. The wisps of a relaxed saxophone unravel under the rain.

Her spirit flips through the treasures of her life, picked and stashed as moments. The shelves of books hold keys to worlds and emotions from all over time. No wonder she has a propensity to get lost in her thoughts. On those trains she rides on knowledge that lightens her lenses on life.

Past loves are not ends. They are lessons, leaving deep roots with origins that fade over time. Those thoughts never really go away, even as minds mature and emotions evaporate. The city a snow globe that contains the flurry of flashbacks.

The last wisp of the incense tumbles into air. A dog barks one more time for good measure before being brought in from the cold. The last car on the block pulls into its driveway and families reconvene for the evening. Another cone of incense is lit, the tingle of clove invigorating her fingers as she begins to type . . .

[Scene]

129

JOSHUA FYE (Jefferson)

On May 30, 2020, our city erupted in a fury fuming from race issues that began centuries ago and have overflowed into the present. Three days later, after marching alongside this city, my wife and I sat on the front porch. We witnessed civilians drenched in black clothing clenching signs with fierce and urgent messages written in bold black ink. These unfamiliar protesters walked past our neighbors, who were out in their yard intently watching exactly what we were, although each of these neighbors may have been watching for different reasons.

We streamed the local news on our phones from the porch. As helicopters hummed over our heads, we continued to watch their feeds showing us one block away, portraying the pain and sorrow being protested over the phrase "I can't breathe." These protesters began to gather outside of the first district police station in order to declare their grievances with the current state of the nation. Their numbers weren't overwhelming, maybe one hundred, but it was enough for military presence, rooftop guards, and helicopters.

The diversity of my block has not been overlooked or underappreciated, mixtures of backgrounds who socialize with one another on sun drenched evenings in the cool spring or sweltering summer heat. Elementary aged children on their brightly colored bikes joyously screaming and chasing one another down the middle of the broken pavement most nights of the summer. Neighbors drinking either out of need or want as they play games on the sidewalk or others continuing their never-ending lawn improvements through dusky spring evenings. Yet on that golden and humid day, everything felt different. The military tanks visible from my porch at the end of the block and the constant rumbling of police motorcycles and speeding police vehicles up and down our street brooded over the neighborhood creating a heavy and daunting presence. There weren't any bliss-filled children on the street that whole evening.

Pictures were posted live on the news of the corner store located directly on the other side of my block; store owner with folded arms, rifle strapped over his shoulder and chest, ready to defend his business. As I drove home earlier that afternoon, I saw one of the many small car lots that litter Lorain had removed their inventory and replaced their presence with heavily boarded windows. Fear had overcome this far corner of the city. The news continued to show images of National Guard and police presence on the rooftops as chants of George Floyd's name rang in the streets. The march began that afternoon and carried down West 130th right behind our house.

The neighborhood was in movement that night with many people out on their lawns reeling from the tensions from that day and days prior. Quietly a protester sat in his car on our street texting. This action to the distraught working-class neighbor across from this car deemed it a threat to his livelihood as he began to verbally berate the protester screaming at him to leave. The protester with his black shirt and black skin responding with equal frustration. Screaming back at the neighbor, throwing hands and fists out of his used car attempting to make his point and pull away to safety at the same time. The neighbor surpassing the level of anger being brought to him through volume that carried the whole block as multiple neighbors walked off their porches to witness the strain and tensity on display. The used car sped off driving while being chased down by the neighbor in his blue jeans and tall beer in hand.

The words of our nation's leader the night before and the ominous militaristic existence on the block muted my desire to march alongside our city that day. I felt my voice stifled by fear I have not had to confront yet in my lifetime. Advantages and freedoms I've been born into allowing me to choose when I get to put myself in uncertain or threatening situations unlike those who I want to call my brothers and sisters. A peaceful march by those unknown dressed in black and chanting phrases that carry their hurt and frustration. They marched until midnight from 130th to 105th and back, continuing to march into Lakewood and back yet again.

The beauty of the neighborhood diminished ever so slightly that evening. But only momentarily. An ever evolving and fluctuating love and hate that comes with living in a city. So many variables contribute to the allure and frightfulness of an urban landscape, specifically one fraught with its own convoluted history. Hope creeps in shyly but is easily startled. I look to the emphatic neighbor that cuts my yard without even asking, I look to the always generous neighbor who I gave my old couch to, I look to the gracious neighbor who openly invites anyone and everyone to play a game or two on his front lawn, and at the stunningly forgiving children who coalesce on our block every evening as parts of this city clamor to drive forward and other pieces fearfully fight to look back.

Lincoln Park Love Letter

LINDSAY SMITH (Tremont)

Summer evening, mid-July,
I wave once passing by.
Dogs on a leash, a family of squirrels,
All basking in this beautiful world.
This love is different, can't you see.
What's more loyal than these trees?
Sprawling sidewalks, a set of swings
Blooming lilies, pretty things.
Church bells ring as we walk through
The farmers market to get to you.
Soft green grass tickles my feet,
At the picnic table I take a seat.
As I look around, with so much to see,
I realize these feelings do not belong solely to me.
It's the center of our neighborhood we all come to,
Lincoln Park, here's to you.

My Cleveland Story

ANDREW SYKALUK (Downtown)

Everyone knows about the movie *A Christmas Story*, but not every Clevelander knows that Bob Clark wrote a sequel called *My Summer Story*, also known as *It Runs in the Family*. I always joke that I did my career backwards, got into acting and then became a food worker. Normally people do the opposite.

In the spring of 1993, my cousin Diana, in her early twenties, finished her acting degree and told her mom that she was heading downtown to audition for a role in an upcoming movie to be filmed in Cleveland that summer. Her mother suggested that I should come too. I was only seven years old with red hair, blue eyes, white eyebrows, and a charming smile. Diana agreed. My mother, Anna, overheard the news and told Diana that she would drive us. The three of us got in my mom's 1986 red Honda Civic and headed to 1127 Euclid Avenue.

On the way to the building, I annoyed my cousin with questions. "What questions will they ask? What roles am I up for? Will I get paid?" Diana replied with "They will ask you for your name, age, and location. As far as roles, they have lots that need to be filled." She didn't answer the third question, or if she did, I didn't pay any attention, as I became distracted by birds flying and people walking outside the window.

We pulled up to the brick building on Euclid Avenue. My mother held my hands so I wouldn't wander off, and we went inside. On the third floor, we entered a room with walls white as eggshells, the chairs black as charcoal. To brighten the room, there were hints of green plants. The waiting room smelled of hairspray and perfume. We went to the front desk and told the secretary that we came to audition for a movie. The lady pointed to a spot in the corner near the entrance. Diana went in by herself; in about thirty minutes, she came back. About an hour later, they called our names. Four people sat at the table, one of them took individual shots of my mom and me with a Polaroid camera. Another person videotaped us. The third person took notes, and the last one asked questions. The person with the camera asked us to stand on the red X on the carpet. The guy asking questions took Polaroid pictures and said, "Please look in the camera and state your names, age, and location. One at a time please."

I went first. I said, “My name is Andrew Sykaluk, I am seven years old, and we are in a building.” The man said, “What city do you live in?” I answered, “The west side of Cleveland.” The person taking notes took the developed picture and wrote that on the photo. My mother was next. She said to me, “Andrew, plug your ears.” I did what my mother told me. She didn’t want me to know that she wasn’t twenty-five years old. At the end, we were asked to line up and smile at the camera. That’s when my mom and I noticed that the man taking notes separated our pictures from the rest.

We headed to the elevator and my mother said, “I don’t think we’ll get the part, but at least we got experience to audition.” At home, the phone rang, and it was the realtor about a house that my mom put a bid on. She then said to me, “Good thing we didn’t get the part because between moving and doing the movie it would be too much for all of us.” A minute later, the phone rang again. Judging from the conversation, it wasn’t a friend or about our soon-to-be home; the agency called to let my mom and me know that we got the job. My mom was cast as the porch sitter, and I had two roles, a hillbilly and a schoolboy. My mom called her sister to see if Diana got any parts in the movie. Sadly, she didn’t get a role.

During the summer of 1993, a week before shooting the movie, the staff told my mother that before going on set I would need to get a pair of white shoes and make them dirty. We went to Kohl’s and got K-Swiss shoes in size 1½. At home, she took the shoes and lathered them with soil from our garden while laughing that we had to get them dirty.

On the day of shooting, we arrived at the area where the Jacobs Pavilion at Nautica is now. I wore my proud dirty shoes and had on a Mickey Mouse t-shirt and shorts. The area that we were in looked like a desert somewhere in Africa; no stores, just a tent with metal folding chairs and cold wooden folding tables. While waiting I chatted with other kids my age and also other adults. Mostly the adults would say, “You are so cute,” then pinch both of my cheeks.

A white Ford van pulled up to the tent, and a man in a polo shirt with a clipboard stepped out of the van and called out names. I screamed, “MOM!” My mom heard that and came to get me. We then headed to the front of the line and when they called my name, my mother had to go with me because I am a minor. The windows in the van were tinted, the car had that new car smell, and my hands were sweating due to nervousness.

We headed to a parking lot nearby with trailers all around. I had to look the part before heading to the set. In the wardrobe trailer, there were tons of clothes; it looked like a hoarder lived there. I headed to the bathroom, and the lady gave me clothes to try on. The outfit for the hillbilly was a potato sack shirt and dirty-looking jeans. For the schoolboy, they gave me a brown striped shirt and a different pair of jeans.

One day I got to take a picture with Mary Steenburgen and Charles Grodin after the shooting. This movie provided me with an agent, and I got to be in another movie, magazine ads, and commercials. My modeling career ended when the agency went bankrupt. Cleveland gave me the opportunity to try something that I would never have thought of, and I am grateful for it.

Faces of Change: Black Flight in the Wake of Jim Crow

DAVIDIONE C. PEARL (Near West Side)

From the depths
Of the sweltering south
Following industrial promise
Salt Caves and Molten Steel
On the heel of succession
Hot muskets and caved plight
Emerged black collar migration
Enduring families assured
Wandering familiar wilderness
To storied Cleveland shores
Staking claim and provision
In challenging
Unregulated new realities
With dreams to become
What the Crowing haunts of Confederacy
Blistering chattel legacies
And scorched judicial roads from Uncle Tom's Cabin
Emphatically disavowed to pave
That the seed
Of distinct Afrofuturism
Hewn of weathered body
May persevere and rise again out of the nation's ashes
Like Mighty Obsidian Towers
Empowered Unbreakable and Strong
Gazing immovably
Into the unwavering light
Of a firmly Reconstructed tomorrow

The #14 Takes Me Everywhere I Want to Go

DANIELLE N. DIXON (Mt. Pleasant)

The judge gave my granddad an ultimatum.

"You must pick between drinking or driving, but you cannot continue to do both."

Without a word my granddad reached into his wallet, pulled out his license and handed it to the bailiff.

"Sir, are you serious? You would rather give up your license than stop drinking?"

My granddad responded, "The #14 takes me everywhere I want to go."

And, just like that, my granddad never had a license again.

The #14 bus lines ran from downtown all the way out to Sunny Acres. The expanse of my granddad's world existed between those two destinations.

I asked my granddad once why he never left the hood. There was a long pause. He looked at me the way so many older black folks do, with that "other" kind of knowing. This knowing is a life-sized blade on a pendulum that swings between believing I may be too gullible to understand the problem and hoping that my uninhibited optimism really could change the world. It swings between the possibility of getting killed trying to achieve success in white spaces and wanting to cheer me on to see if I could achieve success in white spaces. The blade swings so close to my head sometimes that its wind rustles my hair. It swooshes past as I talk of leaving the hood as if it's a place to escape from, when I was benefitting from generational wealth created there. It swooshes past again at the thought that I could trailblaze a bigger reality for us that reaches further than between downtown and Sunny Acres. Could he stand the wait to see how long it takes for the world to cut me down? Or, should he just stab my dreams in the heart now and get it over with? Would the death of my dreams be ruled a mercy killing if it comes from the hands of someone who loves me?

He is guarded before he speaks. He answers, "Why would I go where that I'm not welcome?"

That sentence scratched me like a thousand papercuts from micro-aggressions disguised as jokes. I felt the slap of backhanded compliments, like being told how well-spoken he is for a black man. I felt the weight of being an ambassador for the whole black nation. I choked on all the words he couldn't say in mixed company. Felt the heartburn from all the pride he swallowed with a VO chaser in order to survive those same white spaces. I saw the same pendulum, with the life-sized blade at the end swing between desire and fear in a white woman's eyes, knowing that both could end him. I heard the thousands of prayers black women pray for their sons and husbands to make it back home alive.

The hood certainly has had its battles. But those wars he knew. It was easier for him that the people at home looked like us. At home, there was no one that he had to help catch up to the learning curve, no one to have to explain the joke to. They had whole conversations with facial expressions and eye movements. At home, people understood each other without having to relive the trauma of explaining the bond of their shared unfortunate circumstances. My granddad and his friends were like soldiers who had been in the trenches together. They didn't talk about the horrors of war, what they've lost, who they've killed, or what has died within them along the way. Instead they met up at the local watering hole and commiserated over drinks until they remembered the sound of their own laughter. They were thankful for each other and their small lots of promised land they called home. The media told them that their home was a war zone, but they made sure it didn't look that way. They kept fresh paint on their houses, kept their lawns manicured, and never let trash sit in their neighbor's yard without picking it up.

I supposed if I made peace with our lot between the red lines, the #14 really would take me everywhere I'd want to go, as long as I only wanted to go between downtown and Sunny Acres.

Collinwood Stories, Told and Untold

KAREN GYGLI (Collinwood)

There is the Collinwood on *Dark Shadows*, on Channel 5 every day at four, and there is the Collinwood all around me. It is 1970 and I am seven years old.

This is what I remember about being a kid in Collinwood. It's around 1970, maybe a little earlier, maybe a little later. You know how time and memories polka around each other.

Good, Barnabas Collins is here. Come on, we'll show you around! To fly, you will need to hold onto my hand on your right, and Barnabas' little bony bat wing on your left. Are you afraid? I'm not afraid, I fly with Barnabas a lot. Sometimes even at night!

Yes. I was a very weird kid.

Barnabas is a good vampire; he protects David Collins, the little boy on the show. The Collinwood Barnabas knows best is his old family estate in a spooky forest near a cliff with crashing waves. He travels through time and knows a lot of stories. But I know MY Collinwood. I know a lot of stories too.

You are the seven-year-old Me. You don't know all that much. Grandma, now she knew all the stories. When she was on the phone, she used Slovenian to guard from us the history of neighborhood wars and truces. Occasionally, a spicy tidbit would erupt in English. "Oh, yeah, he knew her alright." "Well, I guess Russia wasn't so great after all, huh?" "And they stayed away from him after that." "At the asylum, yes, yes." But then, she went right back to Slovenian. I didn't speak a word of Slovenian. How was I supposed to eavesdrop?

The Collinwood around me I never see on TV.

The Collinwood on TV has vampires, werewolves, and secret rooms. But the Collinwood around me doesn't have even one ghost or a single possessed animal. It's pretty boring.

My Collinwood had narrow streets named for long ago English battles and poets, filled with duplexes staring each other down, alleys of old brick coffee pot patterns on the backs of garages. Many languages were spoken here, take your pick: Slovenian, Italian, Croatian, Cleveland

English, Appalachian English . . .

See the big Irish flag on Waterloo? That's where Danny Green lives. There's this Chihuahua that lives next door to Danny Green. That dog barks and jumps and yelps every time someone walks by. It's just a stupid mean Chihuahua and nobody likes it.

A few years from now, I will sleep through the bomb that tries to blow up Danny Green in his apartment on Waterloo, a block away from my house. Danny will survive that attempt on his life. My friend Michelle and I will walk to his trailer in the rubble with the big Irish flag out front, although we are warned by parents not to go that way. I'm not sure what we think we might see. No one is around. Nothing happens. If it is hot, not even the Irish flag will budge. So we will walk on by.

There's Lawson's, where we buy banana and grape popsicles and save the sticks to make dolls. There's Betty's Bargains. One time, I bought a vase there for a dollar and took it home to Grandma and she told me to never go back there again, but she wouldn't tell me why.

See? There were a lot of stories that never got told to seven-year-olds. It felt like everything that would ever happen here already did. It felt stuck in the past. The Brady Bunch never lived in Collinwood.

Here is Memorial School, where all the kids died because they didn't have fire drills and doors that swung out. Sister Honora at St. Jerome's School says we are all safer now because we have fire drills and doors that swing out. There is the garden with all their names. It was a long time ago, even before Grandma, and she is the oldest person I know.

I sometimes imagined those kids from long ago, wearing their high button shoes and lace, unsmiling, glaring at our banana and grape popsicles, silently demanding we hand them over.

Yes. I am a weird adult.

We are heading to the best street, East 164th, and as we fly, I will tell you and Barnabas a story. Once upon a time, there was a one-room storefront owned by two brothers who hated each other. On one side of the storefront, there was a butcher, a fat friendly man who smiled as he took Grandma's list from us. On the other side was the grocer, a skinny balding man who watched us with a frown. The grocer would yell at us to get our stuff and pay already, and the butcher would give us a piece of salami, a free sample, just to make his brother mad. The End. That's all I know.

There's the Grovewood Public Pool. I once saw my friend Beth's lips actually turn blue, actually blue, because she was so cold from the water.

We all squirmed on our towels over hot concrete and everything smelled like Coppertone and someone's Donald Duck transistor radio was playing "Free Ride."

There's our playground with huge metal monkey bars, on Grovewood across the street from Humphry's Field. I make a God's Eye out of yarn and sticks when they have summer craft lessons on the picnic tables. The big kids slide down the center pole of the monkey bars, or hang upside down, nothing between their heads and the concrete below. Next year, when I'm bigger, I will slide down that center pole. I'm not afraid. Don't listen to Michelle.

There's Uncle Bill's Discount Store. That's where we go to buy jeans or eight-track tapes or sticky contact paper to protect our phonics books because Sister Honora tells us to.

There was a yellow wart-shaped ice cream stand called Zips or Zots or Zerts, something with a Z. We never went there. Why didn't we go there? That was one groovy building! They had soft serve! It was right next to Uncle Bill's, Mom!

Finally, this is the best place. This is where Euclid Beach is! I ride the kiddie train and the kiddie cowboy ride, and I fire fake guns as I ride around and around on a horse. There are so many trees and you can smell the candy kisses cooking. You can hear people screaming as they speed down the big hill and splash into the water. A robot fortune teller waves her hands jerkily over a crystal ball and a card pops out. Skee-Ball! I'm very good at Skee-Ball!

It's closed up now, no more screaming riders on the roller coaster that soared above the sycamores along Lake Shore Boulevard like a loose Slinky. No more Laffing Sal. What kind of sadistic maniac puts a mechanical chortling woman, grimacing with mirth, in front of little children?

I will tell you and Barnabas another story!

Don't change the subject!

You know, Euclid Beach didn't let Black people in for a long time, don't you? The park didn't allow them to use the pool or the dance hall. There were civil rights protests there, and the Black protesters were hurt by police. You should have been told that story. We should have talked about that. There was all kinds of racial conflict in this Collinwood. We should still be talking about that, not just how fun the Flying Turns were. No one talks about anything, in Slovenian or English, if they want to forget.

Tonight, I'm up late because we just got home from Humphrey's Field. We watched the Euclid Beach rides burn down. All the neighbors from Arcade Avenue were there too. All the fire trucks lit the night red. I won't be able to see the roller coaster above the trees anymore. "Just teenagers playing around with matches," my dad said. "It's been closed for a year, they should just tear the whole thing down already, what's taking them so long?"

There, Barnabas, take us there! There's the lake! Look at the sand and pretty rocks. Canada's over there somewhere. Ghostly waves crash on the shore, just like the Collinwood on TV!

The Collinwood around us in 1970 is teetering on the edge of Cleveland and the edge of Ohio and the edge of America. In 1970, Collinwood seemed stuck in other people's memories. And now it is living in ours, like a ghost.

Here is where Barnabas must leave us! He must fly away before the sun rises, but you and I can take the #39 bus back to my house.

But first, let's sit on the cool sand and hear a distant train and look ahead as the water turns a lighter and lighter blue as the sun comes up. I've forgotten how to make a God's Eye. Remind me. How do you make a God's Eye?

City Girl

SUSAN EYERMAN

(Detroit-Shoreway / West Park)

I grew in the projects in the 1950s and '60s. We lived for thirteen years at Lakeview Terrace, a housing project in the near west part of Cleveland, right outside of downtown. Lakeview Terrace was completed by the federal government's Works Progress Administration (WPA) in 1937. Its dedication was attended by First Lady Eleanor Roosevelt. Cleveland led the way with this model of development to help struggling families find decent, affordable housing.

We were a struggling family. I knew early on where my family stood economically but it never felt like a prison sentence. It did mark us as "project people" to those we met outside our area. My mother was most affected by that stigma and dressed carefully and carried herself with utmost pride.

My parents were separated, and, although my sister and I lived with our mother, our dad was financially responsible and present in our lives. Both were hard-working blue-collar workers, my dad a taxi driver and our mother worked part-time in restaurants. I knew their hard work kept our apartment clean and nicely furnished. We had food and basic clothing but not too many extras. My mother never drove, and my dad had used cars here and there; Sunday rides were a treat. I never did ask how he got back and forth to work each day without a car. We used public transportation and we walked.

Lakeview Terrace still exists today. Many people still walk the north end of West 25th Street the way I did, moving under the Shoreway Bridge into and out of a warren of streets called Washington, Division, Spruce, and Loop Drive that loops all around that neighborhood.

The northbound walk under the bridge signified a welcome home where red brick buildings surrounded by large trees and grassy yards met me. Heading south under the bridge was like walking through a looking glass into my adventures for the day. My mother walked that walk to work with the intent of bettering our financial situation. That walk helped me develop a love for the city, even its grittiness starting at a very young age.

Our earliest walk was to St. Malachi, a parochial school and church located at the south end of "the bridge." Paying the six-dollar book bill each year (our only tuition) was done by saving a little here and there. Uniforms had to last but I had a clean, ironed blouse every day.

Green space and flowering bushes were abundant. Apartment buildings were built in clusters of three surrounding a common-use courtyard where we played. It wasn't a very diverse group. There were a few black families; two lived in our courtyard. One family with two girls and one family with two boys. The girls were really much younger than most of the kids in the courtyard, but the boys were a part of the group for the short time they lived there. In fact, when I was about eight, Eric was the first to propose to me. I gave him a "we'll see" and we continued our regular play. Our antics entertained neighbors like Mr. Gerrity, our downstairs neighbor in his '90s, who watched from his porch on nice days. I ran errands for him. Mr. Gerrity asked me to marry him later. I was about eleven.

We played games like SPUD and Kick the Can. We collected lightning bugs in empty jars with holes poked through the metal lids. The large playground was down a flight of steps from our courtyard, just a whistle away. My mother had a very distinctive whistle, surprisingly loud but sing-song sweet, like a chickadee. Big sturdy swings sets, baby swings in their own area, slides, and monkey bars were the initial draw. Once we moved away from adult scrutiny, we hopped over the fence to play war with the boys. Later, childish games put aside, my best friend and I took our transistor radios to sit on the steps. Bobby Vinton, the Four Seasons, Neil Sedaka, and others sang songs that teased our young hearts to think we were all grown up. We were really so cool!

Once my sister and I were in mid-elementary school, my mother worked downtown during school hours in restaurants, like the Forum and the Colonnade. We became experienced bus riders and would meet her downtown for a dinner treat. Sometimes, just a delicious hot dog at Grant's. They buttered those fancy rolls. We knew downtown at an early age and learned to wander on our own there quite early. It was amazing to walk up and down Euclid Avenue, checking out the store windows. I grew confident and loved what we uncovered in our "gritty city."

Summertime brought hours to explore when my mother was at work. The older we got, the farther we explored on foot. After chores were done, we scooted knowing those precious hours offered endless choices. We had to be home in time to start dinner and be angelically present when Mom got home. And so . . .

We walked. In my early years of exploration, it may have been to the neighborhood drugstore that was in the project boundaries and served the community so well. The little store had a wealth of booty. Big wooden drawers with small toys, like jacks and balls and whistles and balloons. We cashed in found pop bottles to buy a toy or maybe get a Coke from the soda fountain. Plain Cokes five cents, seven cents flavored. Lime Cokes were my favorite.

We might spend hours playing jacks on the curb or walk down the hill to watch the Swing Bridge swing. There was the smallest takeout eatery for workers that sold baloney sandwiches on white bread near the railroad tracks that was north of Lakeview. It had an exquisite wooden-framed glass cabinet of penny candy, Mary Janes, Bazooka, candy dots on paper strips, Pixie Stix, wax pop bottles, and my all-time favorite, Sugar Daddy. Definitely worth the trip.

Older and braver, we ventured on foot to the closest city pool, a two-mile walk each way. Sometimes, our feet would take us to Edgewater Park trekking parallel to the Shoreway. The grassy areas above the city water treatment plant would also lure us for sledding, cardboard sliding, and blackberry picking throughout the year. We stopped in the plant for cool drinks of water. Sometimes on weekends, we walked to the Lorain-Fulton theater for a movie that cost a dime. It had to be a good harvest of bottles for that.

Once we regularly ventured downtown just for fun (often on foot), my path to adulthood seemed forged. Uncovering the wealth and beauty of the main branch of the Cleveland Public Library was life altering. Our previous library experience was the traveling library van that came to the neighborhood. Selection was limited due to space, and I read through my age-appropriate "shelf" of books quickly. The librarian had to okay borrowing books from other "shelves."

We felt and acted so grownup when we went into the beautiful Higbee's or May Company department stores. Those were the stores we visited most often since they were on Public Square. It was evident that hard work would enable us to actually shop there one day.

I chose to go to St. Peter's High School that was downtown at East 17th and Superior. Tuition was $110 a year. It was an effort to afford it. I contributed babysitting money to the monthly payments. My parents' sacrifice bought me the ability to learn to support myself.

We moved to an apartment close to the Cleveland-Lakewood border in my senior year. I had a part-time job on Saturdays, and my mother worked full-time. We were making too much money with my dad's support to live at Lakeview. The move was bittersweet. I left some of my long-time friends. That last trip under the bridge was the ride to a different type of living, better by some standards. We worked just as hard, but my mother glowed with pride to move away. We had walked ourselves into a different city life, a good one. I stepped away from the child's view of adventure and longing to real living, working, and enjoying what my gritty city had to offer.

The area I scoured on foot years before had fallen to ruin in spots but was re-developed into a mecca for entertainment in the late 1980s and early '90s. Decades after I left Lakeview Terrace, I took a job with a developer of Cleveland's West Bank of the Flats. I see that Lakeview still supports struggling families. Urban development flourishes down the hill and just past the bridge from it. Walkers still move back and forth to home under that bridge. I pray their walk brings adventure and exploration of the city we call home.

IV. Our Neighborhoods Are More Than Home

There's a Highway Running Through My Yard

DEBBIE MORRIS (Near West Side)

FOR RENT
Detroit-Shoreway Area – Two bedrooms down. Kitchen, bath, living, and dining room. Yard. No Pets. 7926 Grace Avenue, Cleveland, Ohio 44102. Call for more information.

My dad rents the house in the spring of 1962 when I am six years old. Dad, Mom, and me (baby brother, Davy, is staying with relatives in Pennsylvania until September) move to Grace at the beginning of June when school lets out for summer vacation. Grace Avenue is one street south of Lorain Avenue, which is where Universal Drafting, Inc., the machine shop where Dad works, is located. We rent the downstairs half of a two-family home built in the early 1900s, with a front porch adorned by a massive honeysuckle bush. When in bloom, it imbues the entire house with its sweet scent. The house sits on a lovely tree-lined street, surrounded by other two-family homes that are owned by a diverse community of first- and second-generation German, Irish, Italian, Romanian immigrants. In most homes, the grandparents live downstairs, with parents and children occupying the upstairs suite. Only two or three neighbors rent to non-relatives. Everyone seems to get along or keep to themselves.

The street itself is heaven for a six-year-old who has been in the house for the past year. Mom hurt her back in an accident at work, and for the past two years, she has spent most of her time in hospital. When she is home, she is resting, so I lcarn to play quictly in my room. Dad is either looking for work, at work, or at the bar. But Dad getting the job at UD, finding the house on Grace, and having a car that runs more than it breaks down is a rare blessing, especially for me.

However, about a month after we move in, everyone in the neighborhood receives a letter from the state of Ohio. "They want to build a highway, right here," Mom tells Dad when he comes home at lunchtime. The developers plan to buy all the land on Grace, and the other streets close by."

"Do we have to move again?" I ask, alarmed, in between bites of my bologna and ketchup sandwich. "In about five or six years," Mom answers. To a six-year-old, five years is a long time. I promptly forget about the letter, finish my sandwich, and head outside to play.

That summer, I make my first real friends with the other six- and seven-year-old girls in the neighborhood. We take turns playing Barbie on one another's front porch. One of the girls has a new two-foot pool in her backyard, and each day she can choose one person to join her for a "swim." Sometimes I play by myself. I learn to ride my red twenty-inch bike without training wheels. I tie my very own skate key on a shoelace around my neck, put on my metal shoe roller skates, and skate the whole afternoon going up and down the sidewalk on metal shoe skates. When it grows dark, I catch lightning bugs in a glass (yes, glass!) jar while my parents watch from the front porch.

September comes, and on the Wednesday after Labor Day, school starts. Mom enrolls me in the second half of first grade (I'm a January baby) at Halle Elementary School. My small world is growing. I walk to school by myself; up Grace Avenue, to West 79th street, left on West 79th until I make a right onto Clark Avenue. I cross Clark with Mrs. Schneider, our school crossing guard and neighbor (she and her husband live across the street), walk up West 82nd (?), and left on Halle and my school.

I love school, especially reading. Dick, Jane, and Spot. I want to read more, but my school does not have a library, and my parents do not have the funds to buy me books. Miss Hayes, my teacher, teaches my class about the library. The library is where children and adults can go to borrow books if they promise to take care of them and return to the library on the date due. Miss Hayes says there is a library not far from the school, the Lorain Branch of Cleveland Public Library. Miss Hayes gives us a form from the library that a parent must sign if we would like to borrow books with our very own library card. I run all the way home after school to tell Mom all about the library and library card. She promises that one day very soon, I can visit the library and get my library card.

Soon it is the end of September, and Aunt Dee, Uncle Tom, and my cousin, Sheila, bring Davy home. They are moving to Cleveland to help Mom care for Davy, who will soon be one years old. Sheila is fourteen, and on the day she enrolls at West Tech High I get to stay home from school. Our dads are moving bedroom furniture around to make room for everyone to sleep. Although we are trying to keep out of the way, we are not doing a good job. I see Sheila and Mom talking and watch as

Mom hands her a paper. Sheila puts on her jacket and walks over and gives me a sweater.

"Do you want to walk to the library?" she asks me. The library? Yes! I am going to the library! ME! I am going to the library! I run out the front door and down the steps, turn and wait for Sheila; I realize I don't know my way to the library. We set off walking westward on Grace with the first of autumn's fallen leaves crunching on the sidewalk beneath our shoes. The sun is above us, but the air is chilly, and there is a slight breeze coming from the direction of Lake Erie. We reach West 83rd Street and turn right. After a few steps, I see the library! It's so close to our house! It's beautiful! Sheila takes my hand, and we cross Lorain Avenue. Usually, I would argue that I am too big to hold hands, but today I don't mind. We walk a few more feet, and then we are climbing the concrete steps toward two large wood-trimmed glass doors. It takes both of us to open the door. Once inside the room, we stop for a long minute to catch our breath and look around.

There is a small table up ahead on the right that holds small sheets of lined paper, and a pencil attached to the table by a string. In front of the table, the circulation counter encompasses the center of the room. It is made of wood and sits between two floor-to-ceiling white columns. The counter forms a large square, and the library staff works behind the counter. Wall-to-wall bookshelves filled with books lines the perimeter. Above the bookshelves, both side walls have three large windows filling the room with natural light. Behind the circulation desk, there is a mural of what I now know to be Ohio City looking towards what will one day be Downtown Cleveland. We walk over to the circulation desk. Sheila asks a staff member who we see to apply for a library card. She directs us to the children's room on the right.

"Oh!" I cry out, and Sheila shushes me. This room also has natural light coming through windows. Afternoon shadows dance on top of child-sized tables and chairs. I walk to the middle of the room and slowly turn in a circle. A fireplace adorns one wall with books displayed on the mantel. There are bookshelves around the perimeter of this room also. In the back corner stands a flannel board with the words "Story Corner" at the top and pumpkins on the side. Books are everywhere. Even at six, books are my heaven.

"I'm Mrs. Fedas, the children's librarian," a kind voice says. "May I help you?" I turn around, and Mrs. Fedas is looking at me, smiling. Mrs. Fedas is a short woman, with kind eyes and a welcoming smile. She wears earrings and high heels, her dress is pretty, and she smells nice. "I would like to get a library card." I hand Mrs. Fedas the form. Once she sees my mother's signature, she motions to me to follow her to a small office in the left corner at the back of the room and asks us to wait by the door. Books, stacks of white cards, stamp pads and stamps, a typewriter, and more, clutter the small office.

Mrs. Fedas returns, smiling, and hands me a brand new, sparkling white Cleveland Public Library Card. I print my name at the bottom. Mrs. Fedas reminds me to keep my library card in a safe place. She tells me that I will need to show it at the circulation desk every time I check out books. She hands me a paper about library guidelines and a listing of children's programs the Lorain Branch offers. Then, she shows me the penny bird.

The penny bird is made of heavy, gray paper. It has eyes and a pointy beak, and two wings with pointy tips. Then she places the tip of the beak on the tip of her finger. She explains that the pennies on its wings help the bird to balance and stay in place. Next, Mrs. Fedas takes a book and shows Sheila and me how to balance the bird on the book. She hands me the bird and smiles her beautiful smile. Her exact words have faded after almost sixty years, but I remember this: Within the pages of books, I can fly around the world just like that little bird and all his friends.

Oh, do I travel the world! I visit Laura Ingalls on the prairie, Mr. Popper and his penguins, Betsy and her little sister, Star, Caddie Woodlawn, and many more! The library introduces me to *Seventeen* and *Writers Digest* magazines. School trips to the library teach me about the card catalog, Dewey decimal numbers, and how I can be a student volunteer in the library when I enter junior high. Most of all, the library becomes my sanctuary. There, I can write and read, and, for a little while, not worry about my parent's fighting, financial issues, and illness. I escape; I travel to the homes of happy families and beautiful places. The Lorain Avenue Library and Mrs. Fedas provide me with a love of books, reading, writing, and libraries.

We rent the house on Grace Avenue for six years. My aunt and uncle both take jobs at Universal Drafting with Dad and rent a house within walking distance, on West 83rd, on the same side of the street as the library.

Sheila graduates from West Tech in 1966, and it is around that time that the state begins purchasing land from homeowners. One morning in 1967, I head off for school at Thomas Jefferson Junior High. As I walk down the street, all of the houses on the south side of Grace are empty but standing, as if awaiting new owners. By the time I walk up the street after school, the houses are razed. A lone oak tree stands in the middle of what is now an empty field. That summer, the neighborhood kids and some of the dads play baseball in the field almost every evening. Some evenings, I sit with Steve, my first love, on the side of the tree away from home base. We joke about driving over this field one day on the highway. We promise to keep in touch. One night he takes out his pocketknife and carves our initials into the one-hundred-year-old trunk. Last fall, I found Steve's obituary in the *Plain Dealer*. I thought about that last summer in the old neighborhood, when nothing mattered but riding bikes, listening to WIXY on my little radio, and the innocence of young love.

By the summer of 1968, the houses on our side of the street are deserted. Some homeowners migrate west to newly formed suburban communities. Some go south and settle in Parma. Others head north to Lakewood and Rocky River, and a few move east towards Mentor and Twinsburg. After four moves in two years, my parents finally purchase a house in West Park. The house is a three-bedroom ranch with a small slab front porch on a tree-lined street named Leroy Avenue. The ranch sits close to the end of the street. The end of the street runs into a field.

And, on the other side of the field, is a highway.

Coming Home

PAMELA ANDERSON (Steelyard)

for Al

Your dad steers with his left hand—right arm
draped across the back of the seat—thumb and index finger
pressed into your mom's shoulder. He maps his territory
as he cruises out of the Ozarks on Route 63—
past the confluence of the two big rivers—and eventually
hitting 71 for that long haul to the place where flames
surge from the stacks in Cleveland's Steelyard.
That's where men crank out three shifts a day—
where your father's life grinds forward
like a slow peeling away of the sky.
From here, it's just a stone's throw
to the old pavilion at Nautica.
You remember the Allman Brothers wailing
their southern rock—small boats drifting
along the Cuyahoga and music filling you up
like a bottle of cold beer on a burning summer day.
Sometimes, coming home
is the only thing that matters.

March 15, 2020

MATTHEW DETTMER (Gordon Square)

Last beer in a bar the one right by my place the end of 76th street before the shoreway they're closing early tonight and will be for a while how long we're not sure the bartender was talking about getting paid with one of the fry cooks about when they'd get their last checks and I honestly didn't feel great most of the day from a late night and after I woke up I laid in bed for a while and then stumbled through a run my fifth of the week and now I'm sipping a brew listening to the way Cleveland people mention tragedy with a drink in hand cracking stale jokes about their lives collapsing, sounds surreal but these are browns fans who flood the streets in twenty degrees screaming with each other at a team that never wins people that realized a long time ago that maybe the definition of winning isn't the same as everywhere else maybe winning is living and continuing to live and that sounds rudimentary but it's true and a week old soccer game was on TV, people would look up at it sometimes forgetting what it was and I took a picture of the last beer and then twenty minutes later realized it wouldn't be the last but the second to last one.

Bungalows

LESLIE KOUBA BEDNAR (Jefferson)

Bungalows. Lots of them. All in rows.
One after the other. Along a brick street. Life unfolds.
Different style dormers. Front doors, many hues.
Garages. Some porches. Large old trees. Some new.

Juan and his wife, young daughter and son.
Generous. Kind. Kid sounds drift by. From the pool and the yard.
Basketball. Rim shot. Lands by our chairs.
Son asks politely. Come get it! We live on this street - with you.

Her mother, her brothers, her long dark hair.
Quiet lives. Roses. Small backyard meals.
The boys have their cars. She has her chores.
Rugs scrubbed and hanging. Our street is their home.

New neighbor. Welcome. Roxana and kids.
Cell numbers shared. A laugh. Someone's always here.
Single mom. One car. Three workers. Three shifts.
She runs. And she runs. In and out of our street.

Castro. Behind us. Works hard. Seldom home.
Shared tree. Can we cut it? Yes, please. Oh, good, thanks.
Mows when he can. Older soul. Cheerful.
Truly our neighbor. But next street over.

Margaret. Dog walker. Plain and polite.
Asks if the fire screen is meant for the trash. Yes, please take it.
Dog barks. So loudly. We give up our chat.
She totes the screen. Down our street. To her home.
Two doors away. Young couple. Blond child.
Names exchanged. Greetings given. But now, I forget.
Instead. We wave our hellos. When we can.
As they raise a family. On our street.

Gloria. Single. Diagonally close.
Here twenty years. Seen some come. Seen some go.
Sits on her front step, surveying our block.
Mother of the street. Queen of her yard.

Now us? We've lived here a year. Two wives. Four cats.
In our quiet bungalow. On our quiet street.
You good? Yep. All good. That's good. There is peace.
In our row of bungalows. On our quiet street.

A Dad for All Seasons

ANNMARIE KELLY-HARBAUGH

(Near East Side)

We found out that Dad had stage 4 brain cancer in November 2017. As a family, we collectively held our breath as we listened to University Hospital doctors tell Dad to get his affairs in order and that folks with his diagnosis had fourteen months to live. As you can imagine, we cried a lot during that time. And we were angry—of all the people, why did this have to happen to him?

But most of all, we wanted to make good use of this last gift of time. We asked Dad about his bucket list—where did he want to travel? Ireland? Greece? What foods did he want to eat? The *zuppa di casa* at Mia Bella in Little Italy? The Reuben sandwich at Slyman's deli? What opportunities had he left undone?

It should not have surprised any of us that he had no such list. Instead, he set about the business of daily living—babysitting his grandchildren, playing hide-and-go-seek with the younger ones and watching the older kiddos play basketball and run track at Forest Hills and Cain Park. He planted cucumbers and tomatoes in his garden, made sure the bird feeders were full of seeds, and trimmed trees near the house in the spring and fall.

Our dad was a magnanimous father. His love for us was a river that overflowed its banks. When my brother, Kevin, was eight, he said he wanted a treehouse. So Dad, who had no woodworking background, went and talked to the shop teachers at the high school, and the guys at the local hardware, and built my brother a double-decker, with a rope swing that allowed you to jump out of the treehouse and swing up over our garage. Most parents would have thought smaller and safer, but when it came to his kids, Dad was all about adventure. He drove all over Northeast Ohio—hours and hours in rain, sleet, and snow—to watch my brother, John, run track races that lasted about sixty seconds. When it came to his kids, no distance was too far. Dad mortgaged his house to pay for my wedding and never told me about it. He took up watercolors with my sister, Jenny, proudly producing landscapes and skylines that he felt, in his words, "an average fourth grader would have been proud of." But they learned to paint together. He made time to learn something my sister loved.

It was not that my dad did not have a bucket list, but rather, as my sister pointed out, we, the friends and family in his life—WE WERE HIS BUCKET LIST. Dad never traveled to Ireland, but my brother John did, and he kissed the Blarney stone for him. My dad never played college basketball, but he lived vicariously through and cheered endlessly for our local teams. Dad never published a book or painted much he was proud of, but I wrote one and my sister has framed paintings on people's walls. Dad never sang a solo, but he watched my brother Kevin belt out many of them, and Dad joined a choir to perform beside both his sons when he retired. They sang the national anthem at the Indians games every season.

My dad was the best father, grandpa, brother, coach, friend, and whistler most of us have ever known. If you learn anything from his life, please learn this: First, love magnanimously—listen to your family, neighbors, and friends. Open your heart and make time for them. Forgive. Be generous of mind and loyal of heart—give people every opportunity to succeed. And, second, be one another's bucket list.

Kinsman Stories

STUART TERMAN (Kinsman)

Kinsman (kinz' man) n. pl men
A relative especially a male relative
Ref; Websters New world Dictionary of the American Language Pg 334 Copyright 1979

Originally named South High, and then called by its present name of Kinsman, this road stretched from Cleveland's inner-city Woodland, a name thought more bucolic, and continued east through the Mt. Pleasant Neighborhood, towards far-off Kinsman, Ohio near Pennsylvania, that was named after John Kinsman, a land agent.

The etymology of this name notwithstanding, it bravely winds its way east past buildings, stores, apartments, churches and the previously named Kinsman Jewish Center that was one of the city's first Orthodox congregations to be organized along non-national lines.

My grandfather was sent to the US by his parents from Poland in 1913, meeting my grandmother who was also sent here by her parents around the same time. They met, married, and, nature taking its marvelous course, were blessed with three children, the youngest being my late mother, with the temple he'd visit now a beautiful and well-used church.

The streets bordering Kinsman were at that time an affordable neighborhood where many Jewish people were settling, where my grandfather found a home he could afford, where I lived for several years as a child, and which gradually changed from largely Jewish/Italian/Caucasian demographics to the present mostly African-American population, with the census of people decreasing as the years rolled along. Relatives and families often keeping near their families, indeed confirming the appropriateness of Kinsman's name.

In 1959 or 1960 however, the residents of the adjacent suburban Shaker Heights were becoming concerned about the reputation of "Lower Kinsman," and renamed the stretch of the road within this suburb "Chagrin Boulevard." This name continued further east through Chagrin Falls, Ohio. The more easterly and generally rural communities, being apparently unaware of the distaste that their suburban neighbors had for the original name, were quite happy to continue calling this well paved and well used road by its usual name of Kinsman.

My grandfather was a storytelling pro, with an endless number, most taking place in the pale of Europe or in 1950s Cleveland, usually involving a monkey named Doniel. He'd heard them

from his own grandfather who heard them—where?? And a monkey in 1880s Warsaw . . . who'd have thought?

The Kaiser and the Czar could settle their problems without involving him, and at age seventeen he travelled alone to New York and then to Detroit, before coming to Cleveland where a relative settled.

He sold tires for his uncle at a building on Carnegie Avenue before acquiring a horse and wagon, selling fruit and making his way.

Pa eventually bought a truck, buying and selling scrap metal.

As a child I'd often travel with him on trips through the city, occasionally taking grandmother to a St. Alexis Hospital hearing specialist, where he'd speak Polish and where his humor cleared away much red tape—a skill he brought with him to the new world along with a small suitcase, his parents' blessing, and his own dreams.

When visiting Mt. Sinai Hospital where my mother worked as an RN, he spoke Yiddish, with English being used in a pinch.

How Pa navigated through street with their signs in a foreign language—English being the foreign language to him—let alone figure out how to save up enough to buy a horse, a wagon, a truck, etc., all seem more like fiction. My grandfather appeared older than his stated age in 1952, but a photo taken in 1920 was quite different, showing a well-dressed, powerful-looking young man, holding my then three-year-old uncle's right hand gently with his left, and a much younger version of my grandmother off to the side, holding uncle Al's other hand, her right hand on Pa's shoulder. His polite gaze looking directly at the camera; a man sure of his abilities. My grandmother, from Odessa, was into baking, sewing and not into telling stories except for the one—and only one—I recall. As a child of nine or ten, while playing outside with her two Ukrainian girlfriends, she overheard some local toughs looking down at the three, fair haired/blue eyed children looking like sisters, commenting "none of them here . . ." and riding off on their horses.

She went home and described this event to her mother who related it to her father Simcha, a wary soul, who understood that the " . . . them . . . " included him, and he soon packed up his four children, the oldest daughter Shaindel, age nineteen, being entrusted with getting them to a safer place: travelling here where she met Nathan who'd already acquired the horse, wagon, and suit.

They eventually found that three-story home in the Mt. Pleasant neighborhood of the welcoming city of Cleveland, the place of refuge from the terror that was developing in the beloved homes that they'd both left.

The name of this area, Mt. Pleasant, was derived from its leafy appearance and dramatic views, with Kinsman Road being the main through fare running from the inner city out towards the more suburban Shaker Heights and eastern Cleveland suburbs, and continuing east towards where African Americans were moving to the area that would be incorporated in 1944 as Woodmere, Ohio.

The streetlights near my grandparents' East 153rd Street home shone into our room as Pa would tell me his evening story, occasionally speaking English but more often Yiddish or Polish, though no rigid boundaries existed or prevented this being told in two, or even three, languages. A free flow of the language and story, each with some instruction, till its conclusion, sensible, expected.

The feather-quilt warmly enveloped me along with his heavily accented winters' evenings' story, and I only had to continue these stories for my own children, although the requests became less frequent as each of the four got older.

Our now lovely home is just a few blocks south of Chagrin Boulevard, perhaps just a coincidence although to this day I'm not certain as it's almost exactly the distance south from Chagrin Boulevard, as my grandparents' home was from Kinsman, and the occasional train whistle one hears when opening up our bedroom window is identical to that I'd heard when opening the window on East 153rd, and quietly listening. Perhaps the same train is still at work so far away. . .

Doniel would arrive, occasionally to join the school orchestra to bail out the violinist who'd hurt his hand playing ball or help usher an older grandparent to a front seat to listen to the concert.

He was a role model for good deeds—mitzvot—and decency, with talents limited only by my recollection and imagination. The stories would arrive whenever my children requested them, just as I remembered them always doing.

By age eleven and a half, though, requests for stories by my youngest hadn't come in months, and I wasn't sure if they ever would as his adolescence was now coming up our driveway.

At 11 p.m., the lake effect snow blew horizontally outside. Our neighbors' Christmas tree colors were lighting through our woods and into his bedroom. I said good night, putting my papers away before going to bed, pausing where the beige of his room met the grey of the hallway carpet, hearing " . . . a story . . . ?" Quietly. Clearly.

No question, he'd asked for a story; I wasn't sure why, but then again, why not? I stopped, turned and re-crossed back over the threshold between the carpets—between childhood and adolescence—and sat down on the rocking chair I'd bought at the garage sale in 1987 when he was born. Now dark. Wind outside and the lights just visible between gusts of snow.

The sleepy boy on the bed, covered with his own feather quilt, was indeed suddenly longer than I remembered. Doniel was now sitting in Cleveland Municipal stadium at the Browns-Jets playoff game of January 1987, but THIS time quarterback Bernie Kosar, still peeved about the Mark Gastineau foul, needs reliable help and looks to the stands for someone who could catch a ball in bad weather. Doniel answers, fortunately remembering to have brought his helmet . . . a terrific catch, soon a field goal, and the roar of the fans as loud as the gale off nearby Lake Erie.

A few quiet sounds and Sam is asleep, drifting off as the crowd exits the stands and I leave his darkened room, closing a door . . .

A few nights go by, a birthday with games, laughter, friends and a week passes. Two. More. A few spent Christmas trees appear on tree lawns and the lengthening of days noticed by those paying attention. Doniel was away for awhile, but certain to return since my oldest boy, a Sergeant now back home after six months in Afghanistan, called to say hello and mentioned that his three-year-old son likes bedtime stories.

East 93rd

VICTORIA JOHNSON (Union / Miles)

I live on the major thruway of East 93rd Street. A street that can take you from Miles to Lakeshore. Channing names and numbers along the way. From East 93rd to Woodhill, into East 105th until you reach The Lake. We have lived here twenty years and seen the community change. Some people ask me why we stay here, with crime so high. I say because I have a piece of heaven on my corner. This is a special place, unique in its own way. I feel as though I'm in the country, even with the busy street. I have peace.

Yes, we have crime
Yes, people have lost their lives
Some were never solved.
And now buildings that stood built brick by brick are being torn down.
And I wonder what will take its place
I wish for affordable housing, a community center, with after school programs
to keep our kids from falling through the cracks. More businesses owned by the residents. We are unique for every race, lives and work here.
I want to be the change, by building my dream house on the side street behind mine.
This could be a start to bring Union-Miles back.
No more forgotten land.
For I know that a band-aid on broken pipes will not hold. In time the whole system will fold.
Let's fix it right the first time
And we can have less crime
Ghetto is what they say, about where we live
I don't care how nice it is.
Our house maybe in the ghetto but we don't have a ghetto mindset
There's a difference, between living for change
or contributing to our plight.
I'm watching as beautiful tree parks are being planted,
maintained and growing beautifully. I'm watching new elderly housing and new schools coming alive. Nice big playgrounds with sprinklers during the summer, cooling off our youngest.

Does this neighborhood need work? My answer would be yes. Do we have to move?
That answer would be no.

For this is where I live, I work, I play
and sit in my yard freely and every day.
This is inner city living.
It comes with the good, the bad, and the ugly
But what makes this a place that I continue to live, so right?
We are all in this together.
We come together to right our wrongs.
We are not tearing each other down, but growing into caring neighbors,
looking out for each other, offering a helping hand when needed.
Helping to find and keep the peace we have found on East 93rd.

I Think I'm Missing Glenville

SONYA PRYOR-JONES (Glenville)

I can see and smell your roses, Senoia. They are pink, red, and sweet. They make me feel beautiful and safe. You made a home for all of us. Three generations in Glenville.

Yes, there were a few spotty characters. The old men that hawked as we walked home from school. More and more dope boys. A few that we know.

But here, at 11609 Fairport, I'm safe. It's home. You have rules and expectations, dinner by 5:00 p.m., and not takeout but Sunday soul food made with the love of my grandmother's heart and hands. There were conversations about life, love, and the future. There were responsibilities and chores, limitations and mindful boundaries.

I miss you so much, especially right now when life is uncertain and hard. My mom is trying but she can't even hug me. Damn COVID! She does her best as she talks to me from her balcony on a Sunday morning.

We left Glenville soon after you left the earth. We tried to return with the fourth generation but it wasn't safe enough. We felt trapped by the drugs, the fear and the turning of a blind eye.

I stayed as long as I could, but we couldn't do it alone. I had to save my son. He's grown up now. I'm missing Glenville and trying to return. I'll plant a rose garden. I will place African violets in my window seat. There will be sweet smells in the garden and in the home, red, pink, and royalty purple.

Is it my Glenville without my grandma, Senoia? Will it be the same without you? Can I pick up where you left off?

I'm planting a garden too, bringing beautiful things that are tools for making.

There will be 3D printers, vinyl cutters, design software, and human capital.

I think these are bridges to opportunity and tools for life, love, and a self-defined future.

Let's see.

Starting Again

NAILAH MUHAMMAD (Mt. Pleasant)

On May 26, 2017, I relocated back to a place that with every fiber in my being, I did not want to be. Initially, I fought it, while at the same time knowing that it was something that I was supposed to do. That day, the life that I had built in Atlanta, Georgia, ended. A friend of mine and I packed up the trunk of my small silver Toyota Yaris. Each of us having half of the trunk respectively for our belongings, and we left with our sons. While not quite sure what our next steps would be, we were filled with a guided peace that still resonates within us to this day. I drove away from my home, my husband, the business I had built, and acquaintances that could not understand why the life that I was living was no longer serving me. They couldn't see that in my beautiful home, with beautiful family pictures that lined the walls, there was an energy that was suffocating me. In between the tufts of smoke from the incense that burned and lingered in the air until it disappeared was the painful stench of emotional abuse. A stench that no incense could ever cover up. In between the fibers of the carpet was the residue of tears, and if you listened close enough, you could hear the walls cry.

Upon returning to the Cleveland area, slowly but surely things began fall into place. While returning to Cleveland was not in my plan, I couldn't deny the peace that came over me as I made my way up and down Kinsman Road, my old stomping grounds. Even in the midst of my rapidly shifting life, I found comfort in what most would consider common places, the Two Cousins Beauty Supply Store, the Car Wash, Henry's Dry Cleaning. It was a good feeling that no matter what had changed in my life, those places were still there after all these years.

While getting adjusted, I knew I had unfinished business that I had to attend to. I thought Atlanta, Georgia, would be my last stop, but I was wrong. I had lived so many of my formidable years in Cleveland. Years that brought events that caused me so much confusion, disappointment, and pain, but I knew deep down inside there was a deeper reason for my return that was much bigger than me.

During the years I originally lived in Cleveland, my family fell apart. Both of my brothers mysteriously vanished. They had become two of the many victims plagued by mental illness. Upon my return, I was determined to find them. I found one of my brothers in a group home, struggling with the disease of alcohol addiction. I found the other, on the brink of homelessness, not taking his medication and extremely ill. I spent many days, weeks, and months working to ensure they had the care that they needed. At times, I would reflect on the past and smile. They were so close it was as if they could think each other's thoughts, but their individual illnesses destroyed that bond. They had not seen each other in over fifteen years. As the months passed, they were reunited. They began to talk and spend time together again . . . we all did. It was something I never thought I would ever experience again in my life. My sister even traveled to Cleveland to be with us, to experience family. Something many people take for granted, but for us it was a miracle.

In March 2018, my oldest brother so bravely began his battle with the disease of alcohol addiction. We attended meetings almost daily. He began to see a light and taste the sweet nectar of recovery. I saw a glimmer of hope in his eyes that I had not seen since childhood. For the first time in a long time, he began to understand that he was not powerless. We began to make plans for his future, something that he had stopped believing in. On May 18, 2018, while in the midst of his recovery, he experienced a pulmonary embolism and he died. Just like that, he was gone.

Initially, truth be told, I almost lost my mind. However, after a while, I forced myself to use clear vision. I realized that I could have stayed in my beautiful home in Atlanta with the crying walls and tear stained carpet. Instead, I chose to follow my intuition, and I spared myself the dull ache of regret that would have plagued me had I not been here to experience my brother's final years on this planet. My siblings would have never been reunited, and I would have missed his final smiles and laughs and hearing him say the words "I love you". My leap afforded me a sense of peace that is priceless, and, if I had the chance, I would leap just as high all over again.

V. Cleveland Is Where We Live Regardless

Cleveland Tables

BARBARA G. HOWELL (Downtown)

It's not like all the other places and programs. The women and men from Niger, China, Brazil or the Netherlands may have had all of their orientation questions answered during the four days in Washington, DC, but their experience in Cleveland puts them in a new position.

Yes, just like in all the other workplace cities, they will visit in their State Department sponsored weeks in the United States. They will walk around the tourist spots and meet together at coffee shops and local pubs near their hotel on Prospect Avenue. They will even go to Progressive Field or Rocket Mortgage FieldHouse for an Indians or Cavaliers game just like they might in their days in Chicago or Las Vegas. From the Huron Road office of the Cleveland Council on World Affairs (CCWA), the more than 400 foreign professionals from more than 90 countries each year will meet and shadow young local leaders in all levels of government, at hospitals, schools and industries in Cleveland. It's what they do in cities all over the United States in the International Visitor Leadership Program (IVLP). But, for these young men and women who visit, Cleveland is unique and uniquely engaging.

In Cleveland, and usually ONLY in Cleveland, they get a chance to visit my house for dinner. Or the houses and dinner tables of some seventy other "citizen diplomats" who choose to bring peace one person at a time. At these dinners, the IVLP participants will get a chance to interact with each and with us, in Cleveland, in our homes, on our porches, in our kitchens. Whether they have a home visit, a home-cooked meal, served at our dining tables with our kids, friends, grandkids, and pets. If they are lucky, they will get to clear the table and wash the dishes! Whether the "home" to which they are invited is in Shaker Heights, Lakewood, University Circle, or Detroit-Shoreway, it is probably the first (and maybe the only) time in their lives that these young people—who will soon lead their governments, their countries, businesses and their social service agencies—will see what a basement looks like in a US home. And maybe they will get to see the rooms where people sleep and dream.

Cleveland is different. The young people will visit hotels, bars, sports venues, museums, businesses and government offices all over the United States, but only in Cleveland will they get picked up at their hotels, be driven, four or five of them in a group, maybe, at Edgewater Park for a photo op with the Cleveland sign. They can ask how a home here in Cleveland can be over 100 years old when, in their countries, houses are typical destroyed when old, so new, "better" ones can be put up. They can ask questions to just normal people about uncomfortable cultural differences. Sometimes they will want to help cook and pose with babies. They can tell stories about their kids, sisters and boyfriends.

To be sure, many of Cleveland's "citizen diplomats" have grown their worlds and their "extended" families from these opportunities to host dinners. I can only speak for myself. Two young men from Holland were, at different times, around my table. Since then, both they and their parents have exchanged visits with me and my daughter in the US and in Holland. Bushra, my Pakistani "daughter," insisted she should be part of the cooking for the meal to be hosted around my dinner table after our group's visit to Edgewater Park. From her, I learned a great deal about the importance and methods of Halal food preparations as well as the way the government runs in Pakistan where her father was the Minister of Information. Whether the occasion is a tragedy like the 9/11 destruction or a holiday like Eid or Christmas, we send messages of support back and forth. Thank you, technology; she now gets to talk to and see my two-year-old granddaughter, and Bushra takes me out to celebrate with her friends when she gets a new skill certificate or new job. Someday, I hope to travel to the Far East where two dinner guests—from Timor-Leste and Sri Lanka—await an opportunity to repay my dinner hospitality and to show off their friends from a now "famous" place called Cleveland. The staff at CCWA regularly write that the dinner opportunity is often cited as the IVLP's favorite activity and memory, not just from Cleveland but from the entire four-week rotation through CLE and four other US cities.

What happens across these dinner tables? None of these table conversations stand out as much to me as one that took place even before those Cleveland scripts dotted our lakefront. It was a warm fall afternoon as I drove down the Residence Inn. It would be almost midnight before I would take the four professionals back to their hotel. We clearly and very happily exceeded our 9 p.m. curfew.

Stuffed into my little hybrid were four beautifully dressed but rather silent members of the IVLP delegation from the Indian subcontinent who had been, they politely answered, to three meetings with three sets of representatives from social welfare agencies and bureaus in Cleveland already that day. When it was their turn to ask questions on the short trip west, they asked me, "Why they do this?" The questioner had a tired, uneasy edge to his voice as he explained they been to two other cities earlier in the city rotation and had not gone to anyone's home for dinner.

"You're right," I began. "Cleveland is, maybe, the only one of the State Department host cities which uses citizen diplomats to allow our international visitors to see real people and home life here in the United States. The informal nature of the visit gives everyone—guests and hosts—to know each other in a more natural way. Tonight, you won't be special visitors being received and honored; you will be just like any of my other friends who would come to my house for dinner."

Realizing that such casual intimacy was unexpected and a bit unsettling (since most cultures, especially in the government and agency circles in which these three men and one woman ran, were definitely not as informal as to invite prestigious strangers out to dinner let alone to their houses), I sensed I needed to lighten the mood.

"Besides," I cheerfully chimed, "you get to see my basement!"

That promise seemed to turn things in the right direction; they had never dreamed they would be able to see anything in the US besides the "official" side. I have since learned that taking my prestigious foreign visitors to my basement and through the bedrooms is a game changer. They would have the chance they never imagined: to see a real house and how real people lived.

I needed that lightening up as much as my visitors did that September evening. I was actually worried about the mix. Two of the men were from India, one man from Pakistan and the woman from Afghanistan. Tensions were high in the region, and I hoped that those politics would not spill over my dining room table. Two friends were also joining us for dinner, and I was confident that they could sense any rumblings and help me steer the conversation into safe waters.

It turned out that I had nothing to worry about. When we got to my house, they were so tickled about being at someone's home and in someone's neighborhood that the mood turned jovial. The four immediately wanted to have their photo taken together on my front yard, in front of this almost 100-year-old house. Then they wanted me to be in the picture, so the selfie poses started up. We talked about the working-class neighborhood, the age and history of the house, and what a "double" meant. By the time they were choosing seats on my porch, meeting my friends, and munching on carrot sticks and pear slices, they were sharing stories about their homes and neighborhoods, the multistory apartment buildings and the pollution. Reaching across the table to refresh their appetizer plates and glasses of iced tea, it was obvious that they had discovered they had a lot in common with each other, something they really hadn't recognized even though they had already been together for two weeks.

They talked about need and plans for redevelopment, for improving the plight and education of females in their societies. My friends and I shared our similar concerns. Jokes began to circulate about one of the four talks too much and tries to ingratiate himself with every official he met. I taught them the term "kissing up," and worked in a few other slang points. They began using the terms randomly, even if they really didn't describe the current situation, just because they thought they were "cool."

The clock was ticking. While I was relieved and invigorated about how well everyone was getting along and how much we were sharing and learning from each other, it was time for dinner. I mentioned that I was going inside to put the final touches on our vegetarian meal and rose to leave them with my friends on the porch and the carrot sticks. It was at that moment that I absolutely lost control. In a very good way.

One man from India assured us he was a great cook and proffered his services to "flavor up" the rice dish. Not to be left out, the Afghani woman insisted she could help, too. I did not NEED any help, but, suddenly, the dinner preparation was out of my hands with the Indian official demanding more spices and the woman literally raiding my refrigerator! My hundred-year-old, eight-by-twelve-foot kitchen was now overflowing with five people from four countries bumping elbows and butts.

The laughing continued as the dinner was finally pronounced—NOT by me—to be ready. There were lots more family stories and lots of familiar grousing about the ineffectiveness of each and every one of our governments. They proposed ideas and built off of each other's situations and suggestions. There were many more pictures taken of the IVLP participants, of me and my friends, of the house as they walked through the bedrooms and basement. Of the antique doors, of photos of families which were shared from wallets. Business cards were passed around along with exhortations of, "Let me write this guy's contact information. He's the one you need to talk to about how we do it in my country. Or how we can work together between our countries since we have the same problems. Proposals for business partnerships and vacations. There was a lot happening over the dinner table in Cleveland that night.

During the dinner courses, there were incoming phone calls. I was becoming very nervous. It was after 9 p.m. and the calls had been from other groups of participants already back at the hotel. I called my upstairs neighbor and suggested, LOUDLY, that he come down to take a picture of the group before I TOOK THEM BACK TO THE HOTEL! Pictures were taken; we moved back into the living room, but the conversation remained animated with plans being made for a dinner the next night away from the group. I continued to follow up such good suggestions with “Great! So I can take you back now and you can make plans in the car.”

Finally, I resorted to threats. I declared, “I am going out to my car now. Anyone who is going back to the hotel, meet me in the car.” No one moved until I actually got into the car and started driving away.

They waved me back, gave my friends and me souvenirs they had brought from their countries, and, the second time I went to get into my car, one man followed me. We waited; the others finally joined us. Conversation on the way back to the Residence Inn was full of fun and appreciation. We five made a plan to get together again before they left Cleveland. Invitations to visit and stay at homes and apartments and meet people who we “needed” to meet were extended. The car didn’t seem so crowded. The sidewalk in front of the hotel was filled with hugs and promises.

That’s how we do it here in Cleveland. Not peace by governments. Peace, one person at a time.

Lead Poisoning

CONSTANCE SYLVESTER

(Shaker Square)

Hello my name is Eric Sly
And I've come to give you a reason why
You need to watch where you live and take care
To avoid a lead-poisoning scare.
My story starts when I was three
I got really skinny and kept skinning my knee
Mom noticed black and blue marks on my skin
And wondered how this could have been?
I ran around day and night
Without a purpose and crying with all my might
I didn't understand why everyone was sad
I was out of control and my parents were mad.
So off to the doctor my family went
To find out what the bruises meant
"He has the flu," the doctor said
Take him home and put him to bed.
"Oh no!" my Mom said, "This cannot be true"
You need to give him a lead test to find a clue
Off we go to get a blood test
Wait two weeks and we'll know the rest.
The results came back within a day
Lead-levels so high—that's why I couldn't play
To the hospital we must go
To start treatments—we're scared, we just don't know.
I've never been in a hospital room
I met my roommate; it took away the gloom
I tell my parents they must not go
Chelation treatments start tomorrow.
They X-rayed my tummy and oh what a sight!
I had eaten lead chips and enjoyed each and every bite
They had tasted like candy and were quite yummy
Oh, but alas they made me feel crummy.
The IV drips went on for five days straight

The shots were every four hours they cannot be late
It hurts—I'm sad to see Mommy cry
By being brave I'll get well and the tears will dry.
One trip to the hospital was not enough
I needed three times—it was rough
The food that I would try to eat
Tasted like metal, it was not a treat.
After I got home to stay
My life was changed day to day
Medicine to take and health to restore
I grew stronger and healthier and began to eat more.
I didn't know the harm from those chips
It affects the brain, your nerves, and can land in your hips
It's something that never goes away
You need to keep watch so it won't cause your schooling to delay.
I learned that lead is everywhere
In the dirt, in paint, water, and even in the air
Wash your hands, keep clean take a test
Avoid sources of lead and alert others
Then everyone can be their best.

The Masked Symphony

ROSE CARTER (Larchmere)

A myriad of beautiful colors,
Hiding faces,
Protecting us from the spread of peril.

I see a stunning glory.
Intrigued I wonder what lies beneath.
A jovial smile?
One beleaguered with grief?
A shy flautist?
An ostentatious soprano?
I am watching,
Beholding the beauty of this silent symphony,
Is where I find my peace.

Can Understand, Cannot Speak

LISA CHIU (Asiatown)

Before Cleveland had Asiatown, we had China Town—although in the '70s, it was less like a town and more like a corner. Over the years, more Asian restaurants and grocery stores started to open in Cleveland. In the '80s, my mom started working at Hunan Gourmet, a Taiwanese-owned restaurant located inside a hotel on Euclid and East 36th. English was a second language for nearly everyone working at the restaurant, from the owners to the dishwashers, including the wait staff and my mom.

In the summer between tenth and eleventh grade, Mom enlisted me to bus tables at the restaurant while she greeted customers, answered the phone for takeout orders and reservations, and helped manage banquets and large events. At home, I was accustomed to her always bustling about, whether she was keeping me and my sister in line or coordinating activities with her friends. Mom had a loud voice, a quick temper, strong opinions, and no tolerance for idleness. I tried to shush her in public once. I didn't try it again.

At work, Mom was extra bossy, buzzing about making sure everyone was on task. She introduced me to everyone, and a dishwasher smiled, not bothering to correct her when she told me his name was "Amigo." The chef spoke to me in Taiwanese, asking if I could speak Taiwanese too. I hesitated, too shy to answer him. My mom jumped in, responding on my behalf in direct and efficient Taiwanese: can understand, cannot speak. He laughed and showed me how to cut lemon slices quickly with a sharp knife in staccato bursts. He motioned for me to try and laughed again when I sliced the lemon slowly and in uneven chunks.

Every weekday morning, I tagged along with my mom to work at the restaurant It was a different world for me—a darkly lit, carpeted world of tables, booths, and bizarrely, gazebos. Around 10 a.m., I helped with side work, folding cloth napkins and filling clear plastic pitchers with ice and water. If we were expecting a large party or special event, I would help prepare the banquet room, moving tables and chairs and laying out freshly laundered tablecloths. Then I would hang around the coat check area by the aquarium, in front of the hostess booth where my mom was stationed, until customers began to arrive.

As each party was seated, I quietly approached their table and filled their glasses with ice water, accommodating requests—no ice, can I have some lemon slices, leave the pitcher on the table. I stood in the back of the room and refilled glasses if they were half empty. I refilled and replaced empty stainless-steel teapots. After the customers left, I cleared the tables, placing plates, bowls, glasses and teacups in black plastic tubs to take back to the dishwashing station. I swept up food, usually rice, that had fallen to the floor.

Even though I was meek, inexperienced and slow, the restaurant employees treated me kindly. After the lunch rush was over each day, we would enjoy meals the chef prepared just for the staff, dishes that were not on the menu. I saw how hard everyone worked, on their feet every day for long hours.

One day, a group of boisterous businessmen sat down for lunch. As I approached their table, one of them held up his glass and pointed to it. "Wa wa," he said. "Can I have some wa wa?" His colleagues laughed.

"I speak English," I answered, "probably better than you do." My mom overheard and yanked me away. She apologized to the customers, speaking to them softly with her heavy Taiwanese accent.

Out of earshot, I complained to my mom about their rudeness and condescension. There was more I wanted to say to the men. They didn't know who they were talking to; they assumed the broken English they heard from my mom and other restaurant staff was a sign of weakness, and they needed to be told otherwise. My mom said she understood but that I could not speak to them.

Language would be my weapon, I decided then, and I would sharpen it.

Shoreway Blues

MEGHAN DONOVAN (Detroit-Shoreway)

My commute home is a bittersweet part of my day.
It's sweet to be going home to my wife, my pets, my cozy house,
But I feel a pang when I pass Edgewater.
I miss the beach.
Memories of being a child at my grandparents' trailer
Blend into picnics at the park with sweethearts past and present
And drum circles with my best friend.
Lake Erie, I have not forgotten you.
I hope we will be reunited soon without the separation of my car.

CPL 150

KAREN SHEPHARD (Glenville)

I attended Literary Cleveland's 2019 Inkubator Writer's Conference at the Main Branch of the Cleveland Public Library. Being in the library evoked pleasant memories of spending many hours there as a teenager.

I would ride the #3 bus downtown from East 123rd Street along Superior Avenue to the heart of downtown Cleveland, Public Square. I would then walk the short distance to the library.

Once inside, I would go the card catalog (remember those?) to find the call numbers of the books that interested me. On one particular day, I went to the second floor where books on weird or off-beat subject were held. I was in search of books about yoga, a burgeoning interest of mine. I dutifully wrote the call numbers and took them to the librarian. She looked at them then looked up at me with curiosity. She whispered to me, "Are these books about sex?"

"No," I replied, "they are about yoga."

The look on her face let me know that she thought this was even worse.

She got up from the desk and went to the stacks. I followed behind her as she perused the titles. Unfortunately, we did not find any of them. I imagined, and could almost hear her thinking, "What a strange little girl."

I thanked her, left the library, and ran across the street to another favorite haunt, Schroeder's bookstore. Schroeder's bookstore ceased to exist when the land it was on was taken for the construction of the BP building. I found books there and almost exhausted my limited budget buying them, being careful to save enough for the bus ride back home.

Incidents such as this began to mold me into the person I am today. Yoga is no longer considered weird or beyond the pale. It feels good to be able to talk about it and practice it openly. I occasionally run into "Devil's workshop" comments about it, but not so much as in the past when I first became interested in it.

Day of the Living Dead

CHARLOTTE MORGAN (Glenville)

After the Hough riots, the Glenville shootout, and the end of the Civil Rights Movement, the Vietnam War, and the Disco Era, the post-soul movement begins. Lifeless bodies now roam the streets of Glenville. While politicians in D.C. debate the war on drugs, the number of victims grows. They walk in the street towards the killing field that lies south of my house.

I never watched George Romero zombie movies because I feared that shit would happen one day in my neighborhood. These zombies look at the rest of us as game in the struggle to keep drugs flowing in their blood. Crack cocaine addicts do what they can to recreate feeling that first orgasmic high and, as with all tricks, this is impossible. My little brother Chip said, "Big Tony tried crack on a Monday and by that Friday, he had sold all his stuff for drugs."

Do you understand their need to stand out on desolate street corners illuminated by the darkness that is drug addiction and with lost shame, stare down cars as they drive past hoping to earn five dollars by giving a blow job? How do you feel about "strawberries," a term given to women who turned tricks for a rock?

Can you imagine standing outside the Arab store on Parkwood Drive with your head smashed in and a marshmallow ring around your fried lips, begging?

"Hey, I know that voice anywhere. Charlotte, you look the same. Hey, uh, you got some spare change. I want to go to Abbott's to get a couple of wings." She laughs like we are still friends in Mrs. Clouden's fifth grade music class. I realize it's Jackie Hall; well, it used to be. "Oh, I got jumped behind Scotts, that's what happened to my face." I am ashamed to be in this store. We both know people on crack don't eat.

Businesses before owned by blacks became the Arab store. There are usually drug dealers and users perched outside amidst the trash and broken glass. Often, there is a former alcoholic turned crack addict, a black man, who sweeps and does menial tasks for money. The stores are grimy, the produce spoiled, but you can get a cold Pepsi or forty-ounce Old English Malt Liquor, some loose cigarettes or Black & Mild cigars—even an oversize white t-shirt.

I observe the day of the living dead begins with the migration of crack addicts before sunrise. One day I watched Randy, the middle-aged mechanic-turned-crack-addict from down the street make his pilgrimage. When he comes back, he walks in the street; his gait quickened because he has his buzz, his beer, his cigarettes. For now, he all happy and shit. Instinctively, he turns and sees me.

Like many of the dead in Glenville, Randy's clothes are filthy and tell the story of a lost life. His worn green pants are from days gone by when after getting fired from Ford, he worked as a jack leg mechanic who fixes cars in driveways.

"I ain't got no money, Randy."

"Uh, your father's Chrysler sounds like it needs some back brakes. Let me get that for you. Mr. Morgan never buy no Ford."

"No thanks, Randy, he goes to the dealer to get his car repaired."

He walks away defeated. He will ask me again the next time I see him.

A homely white man once approached me early Sunday morning, his body pencil thin. He asked me if I wanted to buy a weed whacker, and when I commented that I already had one he asked: "Where do you keep it? I want you to get it and plug it up so I can show you this one's better."

"Not interested."

His bug-eyed gaze remained fixed on my garage where he perceived there was a treasure. Was he imagining that glass pipe in his mouth? My ladder and lawn mower were later stolen. Now I watch who walks the street because I realize not only are they walking to score their next hit; they are also casing houses.

Ours is no longer a street with beautiful homes and lawns. Many older owners are dead. We have new neighbors. Barbara and her daughter live down the street towards the East 105th end. She dressed modestly. Her hair was always done. One day she asked my next-door neighbor for five dollars to get her bus pass saying she had lots of appointments at Metro. "I got Lupus Miss Jean. Would you please pray for me? Can I go to church with you next week?" Since bus fare was only seventy-five cents, for her story she got three dollars.

Barbara never paid the money back. For a time, she would walk around the block rather than run into Miss Jean who was in her yard early some spring mornings.

One day, I see an unkempt Barbara marching up the street with the zeal of a zombie. The weight of the atmosphere seems almost too much for her emaciated body, yet she regularly walks up to Lakeview where she exchanges money or favors for drugs. I was traveling to the bus stop. Everyone knew it was dangerous up there. An elderly cleaning woman, who also rode the #40 bus to Cedar Road, openly carried a .357 Magnum to protect us as we waited on the corner of Lakeview and Tuscora Avenue.

"Girl, get your happy ass out that bus shelter. You easy prey for these gang banging suckers," she said. "Now on, you wait for me. Don't come up here by yourself."

Barbara not only pan handled outside corner stores; she conned money out of senior citizens for drugs and even kidnapped her elderly neighbor.

Miss Williams, like many of the aged in my neighborhood, has been abandoned by her children, themselves crack addicts. She suffers from Alzheimer's or bouts of dementia. She lives down the street in a two-family house that begs for attention.

Barbara's family owned the run-down house next door. She would call Miss Williams and ask her for money. Barbara is pretending to be Michelle Sanders, the neighbor who helped care for the eighty-year-old woman. I saw Michelle at McDonald's. She told me the story.

"I found out Barbara put Miss Williams in one of her friends' car and took her to Society Bank." Michelle leaned on a cane. She looked old enough to be my mother. I wondered if she was a user.

Michelle called the Society branch on St. Clair. Apparently, the teller was suspicious when she saw the old woman was disoriented and nervous about taking $500 out of her account. Miss Williams, alone and afraid, refused to press charges against her neighbor.

Years into the phenomenon, one random day, the sister of a classmate of mine came walking down the middle of my street. "You want to buy these steaks? I got fresh thick Porterhouse steaks here," she said to passing cars. As she got closer, I remembered how beautiful she used to be.

"Charlotte?" Her voice was the same. "You remember me, Charlotte?" As she came closer, my heart raced.

"Hey Patricia."

"You still talk to my little sister? You all used to be so corny," she laughed. Some blood dripped down her leg.

I took a step closer. "I haven't talked to Danielle since we went to the last reunion."

She came close enough for me to smell the thawed meat and for me to remember the day that she bullied me into snorting heroin.

Danielle lived in a two-family house up the street on Tuscora. I used to come over to watch *Soul Train* on Saturdays. I heard the *Superfly* soundtrack in her living room. Danielle's family lived that life. I was Danielle's friend since elementary school. In high school, we shared a locker. I was short and scrawny with thick glasses, an obvious target.

Patricia sat on the couch and chopped coke and heroin with a razor blade on a chessboard. When done, she snorted the line. She loved to pick on me as she got high. Then, she would disappear and reappear dressed and ready for the street. Hot pants, halter top, and stacked heels. She dared me to snort a line, and so I did. I remember walking home and sleeping for three days. I was desperate to fit in, so I snorted downers, smoked weed, and hashish; I dropped mescaline, windowpane, and microdots. Seeing Patricia reminded me of my near brush with death.

"You want one of these steaks? I'll let you have one for five dollars," she said.

"No thanks, I'm not eating meat these days."

"Well, you got a couple of dollars for an old friend?"

"I ain't got no money on me, Juanita."

"I'll see your old corny ass later," she said. She turned and walked away.

As the dealer by selling, as the addict by using, so the plague spreads. Removed were the landmarks of paradise, and in the field of the fatherless known as Glenville, the dead were found living in run down houses, and apartment buildings. Gang presence and gun violence increased and the soundtrack—that post-soul music—normalized street life. We the poor, ignored, unloved and unprotected were imprisoned.

Sunday Service

DANIELLE N. DIXON (Mt. Pleasant)

Bar-B-Que smoke signals summon Sunday sinners from their slumber
Today, backyard is church
No one is formally invited but every-one will come through
All are welcome in this sanctuary
Come as you are
The gospel of rhythms dusts our blues.
We take communion
Deviled eggs are the body
And the blood, V.O. in red solo
Parishioners bring side dish offerings
Lay them along the altar
Those who can't cook bring plates, cups and ice
Others bring themselves, their love and laughter
Every offering is just enough
There'll be spades and tonk for the kids
But bid whist is grown folk's biz
Half-steppin'
Rise and fly
Slappin' cards and tellin' lies
Turn to your neighbor
Say "Neighbor! It's sacrilegious to renege in this house!"
We commiserate, feed our faces and slap our thighs when we laugh from the gut
We pour one out for our dearly departed
Our time here is short so,
We hug necks and kiss cheeks in this fellowship
There is always a "to-go" plate wrapped in foil
Guests take what they need from the bag of bags under the kitchen sink

The sun bleeds orange across the Mount Pleasant skyline
The breeze carries music and laughter on the wind
We know these are the best days of our lives
This is the day the Lord hath made
Let the church say Amen
Amen.

Where I'm From

KATE BIGAM KAPUT (Cleveland)

After George Ella Lyon

I'm from big, shady oak trees and enough pollen to kill me,
From perennials that survive to find their way back in bloom every spring despite biting frost.
I'm from blindingly hot summer days and feet that blister on the scorching pavement as we let the car cool off after hours spent on Lake Erie.
I'm from kickball on the cul-de-sac as the sun goes down,
And from autumn colors that rival New England's, but with people a hundred times nicer.
I'm from a foot and a half of lake-effect snow with no end in sight,
From no such thing as a day off school if you can still get out of the driveway,
And from digging out your neighbor's car but knowing he'll shovel your sidewalk in return.
I'm from marrying your senior-year sweetheart and sending your kids to the same elementary school you attended, where half the same teachers still teach.
I'm from an aged but familiar face at every hometown dive bar,
And from still—always—identifying yourself by the year you graduated high school because, oh, did you graduate with my cousin?
I'm from a map that leads to small towns whose Native American names you can't pronounce,
From Cuyahoga and Wapakoneta and Tuscarawas and Olentangy,
I'm from the North Coast and summers at Sea World and the best roller coasters in the country,
And flyover towns whose validity and worth are forever being underestimated.
I'm from brown and orange, wine and gold, and nemeses in the form of cities I've never visited,
From that damn Drew Carey song and promising to call it Jacobs Field forever,
From witnessing and jersey-burning and ultimately forgiving,
From "Maybe this year" to "Maybe next year" to "Maybe again someday."
Because I'm from a home that taught us how to hope.

I'm from hard, nasally As that reveal themselves after a few Dortmunders,
From middle class and white trash and never realizing that rich people think they're the same.
I'm from "two hours away" and a hidden cop car on every stretch of highway,
From tree lawns and "needs done" and pop, not soda,
From the candy, the mascot, and the nut, in that order.
I'm from dollar drafts and homemade casseroles and half-priced appetizers,
From Friday nights spent listening to cover bands on the burning river we learned about in history books.
I'm from round on the sides and high in the middle,
And an enthusiastic "I-O!" shouted in return, no matter where else I may roam.

The Street Remembers, or How She Became A Writer

JOANNE LOZAR GLENN (Union / Miles)

Before the lot on East 93rd and Reno in the old Union-Miles neighborhood changed owners only to become vacant decades later, there existed a house. At the back, a rental unit. At the front, a tailor shop. And in the middle, an upstairs-downstairs railroad apartment.

On days when the wind was strong, the father slipped his feet into worn wingtips and ferried his chunky, frizzy-headed daughter down the rubber-treaded stairs to a field at the end of the block, across from a steel mill, where kites flew high.

Other days, when the wind was strong and rain pelted the sidewalk and puddled in the gravel driveway, the girl watched her Red Raven Magic Mirror spin round and round on the turntable while her grandmother tended steaming pots of rigatoni, polenta, chicken wings in gravy. On days like these the girl's uncle was a frequent guest at mid-day dinner. When the mill's whistle blew, he ambled to the house, let himself in, sat at the table. The girl, old enough for kindergarten but home for want of a school bus, marveled at the uncle's perfectly dry white t-shirt and oil-stained dungarees. "I waltzed between raindrops," he'd say.

One night, the girl's parents needed to attend a wake. They took the children—six, three, two—to neighbors who lived across the street above a taxidermy shop. The grandmother, felled by stroke, had died; the children knew only that she was gone. The lady fed them porridge in the waning October light, but they could not be satisfied. When the parents returned to bring the children home, the oldest heaved. Later the middle and youngest would drive their pedal car into a wall. The youngest would cut his head and bleed.

Three winters the family stacked galoshes neatly on the rubber-treaded steps to their apartment. Three springs the parents tilled soil, cultivating the garden the grandmother had started. Two summers the mother sweltered in the upstairs kitchen canning green beans, tomatoes, peaches, pears. Finally the father found a new house in the suburbs, on the corner like the mother wanted, and sold the house to a trucking firm. The family moved just in time to enroll the children in a new school—

fourth grade, first, kindergarten—and to welcome a baby into a room he didn't have to share with anyone.

By then the girl had come to understand her uncle had hidden an umbrella in the entryway on those windy, rain-soaked days. She watched the family grow from five to six to seven, babysat, took refuge in the neighborhood library befriending *Half Magic*, *Pippi Longstocking*, *A Wrinkle in Time.*

The trucking firm razed the old house and its rental unit and tailor shop to erect a building of its own. The taxidermy shop remained dark, except for when lamppost light fell just so on the deer head's antlers and splintered the light into something like a star, sent it shimmering, softly, like the muted echo of a man who waltzed between raindrops.

VI. Parts of a Whole City

Almost a Poem About Shopping

MIMI PEVLIN-FOUST (Shaker Square)

I am trying not to write a poem
about the one-year-old who was killed
by the three-year-old
two days ago in my fair city of Cleveland—
all because someone left a loaded gun
in a house full of kids.

I would rather write a poem
about shopping. People might enjoy
a poem about shopping.

If I wrote a poem about the joys
and challenges of shopping,
no one would have to read
that Braylon Robinson—a baby boy
who was "always smiling"—
died in the ambulance
after being shot in the head.

If I wrote a poem about how
hard it is not to buy all
the colorful dipping bowls at Target,
then I would not have to remember
that Braylon's mother will never
get to buy him a little backpack
for his first day of school.

I wonder what kind of poem
might soothe the heartache
of a nation trapped
in an undeclared war
where too many of us have loved

someone who was shot?
What kind of poem
could stop that heartbreak?
I would like to write it.

A Cleveland's West Side Story

SUSAN POOLE (West Park)

Born into a West Park neighborhood in the mid-sixties, not far from where my parents grew up,

I've always felt a strong connection to my community. There's something about your hometown that never leaves you—it's in your blood. Even when court-ordered busing prompted my family to relocate a few blocks away, crossing over the border into Lakewood to avoid sending me to school clear across town, the feel of our new neighborhood remained the same as the old one. Same kind of people. Same close-knit community.

With age, my memory has become a bit murky, but flashes of my childhood still cross my mind intermittently—like fireflies against a pitch-black sky. It's mostly the faces I see. Of the people who helped shape me into who I am today. Before I was old enough to be influenced by teachers, coaches and scout leaders, our neighbors are the ones who had the most impact on me. The grownups who looked out for me and the other neighborhood kids, to make sure we were safe, well-fed and learning the right lessons from a young age—often times unintentionally.

But let's start with my parents. Thanks to them, growing up in Cleveland was about as perfect as it could be. They worked hard at providing for us, instilled a strong work ethic in all their children, and gave us enough freedom to embrace the joys of being a kid. They didn't burden us with their adult struggles (even though we were at least partially aware of what they were), and they kept a close eye on us while still encouraging and respecting our independence. As a parent myself now, I know how difficult it can be to strike that balance. In the current culture of helicopter moms and "everyone deserves a medal," it's not easy knowing how and when to draw boundaries. My parents never had that trouble.

Looking back, I marvel at how easily and how often my parents simply refused us. Can I stay out past dark? No. Can I sleep over a friend's house? No. Can I ride my bike to Impett Park? No. Long explanations were rarely given, and challenging the answer was a moot point.

There were times when we'd get a glimpse into the rationale behind their decisions. Every time we drove by Halloran Park—and I do mean EACH AND EVERY TIME—we'd hear the story of Beverly Potts, a young girl who went missing from the park and was never found. My mom would launch into a long lecture about stranger danger and gave us the impression that Beverly had just disappeared the day before (when in fact, her disappearance occurred in 1951, when my mom and dad were ten years old). I wonder how many times their parents had recited that same story to them.

One of the benefits of living where we did is that my parents didn't have to watch out for us by themselves. It really does take a village, and our village was ready, willing, and able to step up to the challenge. For starters, there were plenty of city workers living in the area, especially police officers and firemen. If there was ever an emergency, everyone knew who to call.

The landscape of the neighborhood also lent itself to a cohesive environment. Our houses and yards were small, nearly on top of each other. That made it easy to hear your mom calling you for dinner . . . or to overhear one of the seven (yes, seven) kids next door getting grounded for flunking an Algebra test . . . or to spy the lady across the street who used to strip naked while she cleaned her hardwood floors. I guess you take the bad with the good in a tight neighborhood.

Many of our neighbors were like extended family, and we learned a lot from each other. My family is of German descent, so my mom loved to share her sauerkraut balls at Christmas time. The Italian family two doors down always had an extra spot at their dinner table, open to just about anyone, and the Greek family across the street introduced us to things like baklava and vasilopita (a traditional New Year's bread that they'd hide coins inside for good luck).

I spent a lot of time with the Greek family. They had a daughter my age, her mom made the best fried bologna sandwiches, and her dad would take us to the West Side Market on Saturday mornings. That was a real treat for me, as my family only had one car, so we didn't venture out much. While my friend's dad shopped, he'd leave us at one of the stands where a woman named Marge would braid our hair and let us pick from a jar full of brightly colored plastic barrettes (something I'm sure the health department would have frowned upon, and which undoubtedly doesn't happen today).

Beyond the neighbors that we knew by name, there were countless people that simply crossed our paths—random strangers that made an impression on me. There was the clerk at Oriole's, a corner store on Fischer Road where we liked to buy candy, who couldn't have been more forgiving when my mom made my brother and I return the gum that we'd stolen from his shelves. The woman who once rescued me after I fell off my bike—a turquoise Huffy with a white banana seat. I'd been riding alone along the future site of the extended Interstate 90 while they were constructing the McKinley Road exit when I wiped out and skinned my knee. A mom who had been riding with her own kids saw me crying and insisted on walking me home. Guess I'd forgotten about Beverly Potts that afternoon.

One of my most vivid childhood memories taught me an early lesson about the kindness of strangers. My mom was at the wheel of our brown Dodge Dart as we were driving along West 140th Street, going who-knows-where, when it started to pour. Frightened by the thunder and lightning that followed, my brother and I huddled together in the backseat with our eyes wide—no seatbelts of course. If Mom's knuckles had been white, she never let on, choosing to distract us by playing a game of "motorboat." She drove the car close to the curb, speeding through the puddles and splashing water against the windows. We squealed in delight and forgot about our fears—until the car stopped, died on the side of the road thanks to the influx of water flooding the engine.

A cell phone would have come in handy that night, but this was sometime in the late seventies. We were forced to knock on the door of a stranger, on a street that was dark and unfamiliar. I remember thinking how brave our mom was, especially as we were invited inside the home to use the phone and wait until our dad figured out a way to pick us up (remember, one car). The family who lived in the home had been eating dinner, two teenagers sitting on a sofa in front of a console television in the living room, eating chicken and coleslaw from Kentucky Fried Chicken from a pair of wooden TV trays. Their mom offered us drumsticks from the bucket, but we declined; too scared. But by the time we left, it was as if we'd made lifelong friends. The hospitality they'd extended us was exactly the same as any one of our own friends or neighbors would have shown under similar circumstances. That's what you found in and around the Cleveland neighborhoods I frequented as a kid. Good, kind, community-minded people. Always willing to lend a hand.

I don't live close by those neighborhoods anymore, and not all of my recollections are as detailed as some. They don't need to be. They're in my blood. And there are enough remaining landmarks to help jog my memory when I am in the area.

Gene's Place where our high school senior breakfast was held before graduation.

The church at Kamm's Corners where my mom owned a preschool, and the Center for Families and Children right next door where she went to work when we got a little older.

The Public House where I used my fake ID for the first time.

The Poor Clares Monastery—I've always been curious about what life is like inside.

St. Joseph's Academy where my husband and I had planned to have our wedding photos taken until a torrential downpour forced us to cancel the outdoor pictures that day.

And most importantly, Fairview General Hospital, where both myself and my youngest child were born thirty-five years apart. That's especially meaningful, as after I got married, I lived out of state for more than a decade. When given the opportunity to move back to the Greater Cleveland area in the year 2000, we jumped at the chance. The pull of HOME was too strong to resist. But even if the people and places I've named were all gone, they'll always remain in my heart. My husband tells me that I light up any time I run into someone from the "old neighborhood." He's right. There's a connection so strong, but it's hard to describe. Our shared history binds us together forever, reminds me of a simpler time. Perhaps all generations feel that way—that their childhoods were less complicated than the times they grew into. Or maybe that's just what happens when you become an adult. You see the world through a different lens, moving from a sense of freedom to obligation; from feeling safe to providing protection. And perhaps this generation will reflect back on cell phones, video games, and weekends packed with structured activities where everyone gets a medal the same way I fondly reminisce about neighborhood block parties, freeze tag and kick-the-can, staying out until the streetlights came on, and riding my Huffy through the streets of West Park.

Photography Student

MARCIA CAMINO (University Circle)

Say, first thing, a gray day color zap.
Plastic daisies in a bucket on an un-shoveled porch.
You pull from your parka your Minolta and shoot.
Oh sunflower sunflower how yellow you are.
Remember that road trip, that mile-long field?

Say now you tour the museums' grounds.
Imagine chalk art under snow-slush walks.
See Schreckengost's dinosaurs
Vandalized Rodin
The icy lagoon. That willow. Shoot.

Third stop, to warm and micro-aim
The botanical gardens' hothouse one
Orchid a "Purple Rain" hue. Stop Four
Homage to the tie-dye ghosts of Hessler.
For now you shoot their frosty brick street.

A wind rises up. Stop Five Severance Hall.
We ran that time from L'Albatros, right? And
We still missed the start of Wagner. Stop Six
The Barking Spider
But now without friends

Wood burner, burnt-orange, heavily graffitied
Whiteboard restroom walls. Desk lamps
On the bar. On to Mama Santa's
Checked tablecloths, spaghetti, bread.
Where did we fail? Please help me see.

Then dread, facing dusk, up Mayfield
The stone wall, amber-lit, fires.
All in your eye and heart the fading
Lake View Cemetery's blacks and ecrus. But

Tiffany Chapel's stained glass
And some bird in a red-berried tree.
So you fly back down to Murray Hill. Home.
"Tangled up in Blue" plays in your head.
You're that, and that, a balladeer gone rogue.
Your camera's gone warm in your coat.

And what of tonight in your dreams' azure walking?
What guidance through their cold steps can no f-stop claim?
And what of tomorrow when you trek to the proving
Ground of the holy lonely?
The light, the truth? The darkroom.

The Runner

MARIA MIRANDA (Edgewater)

I think of her from time to time now. When I am doing mundane things. I wonder what she buys when she shops for groceries. I wonder what she listens to on her commute to work. I imagine her shopping online, sipping wine with the TV on for background noise. I wonder if we have passed each other in the grocery store or stopped at the same time at the same traffic light before getting on the Shoreway. I like to picture her life colored in the tans and beiges of regularity. I think about her dreams. I hope, that for her, they are vivid, whimsical technicolor fantasies. Her brain wringing out her subconscious for the day. Most of all, I wonder if she still runs.

> *"The Cleveland Division of Police Sex Crimes and Child Abuse Unit is currently investigating a rape which occurred on Tuesday, September 2, 2014, at approximately 5:25 on West 104th Street near Lake Avenue. The victim, a 46-year-old female, was jogging on West 104th street when a male ran up and attacked her from behind, knocking her to the ground in the street. The suspect punched the victim several times in her face and body and pistol whipped her before dragging her behind a building and raping her. The suspect then fled the area on foot." —clevescene.com, September 17, 2014*

Her attack was caught on camera by the condominium's security cameras on West 104th and Lake. Her rapist came from out of some bushes and dragged her into her nightmare. Local news stations played the footage over and over in hopes that someone would recognize something, anything that would lead to his capture. A $10,000 bounty was placed on his head. They never revealed her identity, and despite this she became more than a stranger to me.

Only the trees and the facades of well-to-do homes saw the truth that morning. It felt as if the trees would whisper to me as the wind blew on dusky evenings. *He may be waiting for you. Hurry inside. Have your keys ready in your hand. Be alert at all times.* I could hear the voice of my late mother chiding me for wearing the wrong thing. Her hands wringing until she got a call from me that I made it home safely.

It wasn't as if I didn't know that most sexual assaults are committed by someone the victim knows. I know the statistics. I volunteered for the Cleveland Rape Crisis Center Hotline. But he took her down like something out of a nature film: a beast taking down its prey from behind. Lake Avenue became the Serengeti. Who was next? What would I do if it happened to me?

> *"'There's a lot of people running around here by themselves,' Shoemaker said as she walked her small terrier. 'Maybe people should pair up, or more police. I don't know. The world's becoming a very scary place.'" —Cleveland.com, September 9, 2014*

Man-on-the-street interviews expressed surprise. As if the world wasn't already a pit of despair. This neighborhood is supposed to be safe. We have million-dollar homes on the waterfront. Wine bars. A park. There is a parade of dogs and babies that make their way up and down these streets every day. Why us? The sheer brutality of the crime left people feeling open, vulnerable, angry, and helpless. There was a level of indignation that sat between the lines of hefty mortgage payments and block club calendars.

I can't help but raise an eyebrow when people are surprised to find out that crime happens in their neighborhood. One news story said residents were "stunned." I was never stupid about the probability that I could be the victim of a crime. Fuck adjacency to beaches, pet boutiques, and wine bars. This, however, really hit me hard. For the first time in my life, I felt unsafe. I double-, triple-checked locks. I ran from my garage to my door. I begged my landlord for security lights. I thought about *her*. Constantly. I wondered if her bruises were healing. I wondered if she took time from work. I wondered if she wanted justice.

How long was he to be on the prowl? Some women ran at all hours in defiance. Tracing their route up and through Lake and Edgewater, winding around West Boulevard and back down to the lake. Middle fingers to the wind. Headphones firmly in place. I placed a picture of an armed woman with a shotgun in my front window. I felt like it served as both a warning and a call to action. I kept a baseball bat close to my bed and my rifle, the only firearm I owned, even closer.

Neighbors organized a vigil at the site of the attack. I walked down from my corner across cracked sidewalks, passing manicured lawns in the brisk fall air to a crowd of people holding candles. A quiet anger permeated the silence. A man who came with his girlfriend made the grave mistake of telling women to jog with a partner. A Black man talked about how he feels like he's being profiled by the police. Another resident complained about a homeowner who doesn't keep his bushes maintained, which creates a horrible blind spot for drivers and pedestrians. Candle wax dripped down my hand. Where is she right now? Does she know we're all here in her honor? I was surrounded mostly by people who I had never met, but we all shared a sense of place. *Why didn't I do a better job of knowing my neighbors?* This was our home and for the women, especially, we were under attack. There were dogs on leashes and soft *hellos* and *how are yous* between those who knew each other. The truth hovered thick above us. We weren't special. We weren't immune. We were never safe. The crowd eventually dispersed, and we returned to our homes, locks clicking in place, blinds being drawn.

I thought of him often, too. I wondered where he slept. What he thought. What drove him to do what he did. Something is wrong with him, but does he see himself as normal? Does he live around here? He attacked her in the same place he found her and likely escaped on foot. He must not be far. Have I passed him on the street? Has he walked by my house? What does he eat? He must have moments of normalcy despite being a monster. I wonder what fear looks like to him.

> *"A man was arrested in connection with the rape in a Cleveland neighborhood earlier this month. The suspect was identified by the Cleveland Division of Police as James W. Daniel III of West 104th Street. The arrest was made on West 87th and Lake." — fox8.com, no date*
>
> *"The man dubbed the 'Early Morning Rapist' for recent pre-dawn attacks against two women on the West Side, was arraigned in court Wednesday morning on charges from those two rapes as well as a 2000 rape linked to his DNA. James Daniel III faces 22 counts, including six counts of rape, seven counts of kidnapping, four counts of aggravated robbery, three counts of having weapons while under disability, one count of felonious assault and one count of aggravated burglary.*
>
> *The judge set a $1 million bond." —wkyc.com, October 1, 2014*

He was arrested around the corner from my house. Around the

corner, at a place where I have walked numerous times. The relief washed over me in a warm flush followed by icy shivers. He was as real as she was, and he was caught. He was no longer a phantom haunting our neighborhood. I held my keys in my hand a little looser. My pace was a little more relaxed from my car to my door. I kept the poster in my window until the day I moved out. I remember taking it down, the tape frayed from weather and I thought of him, then I thought of her. I worried about the justice system process and what she'd have to go through. I hoped that she had someone to hold her hand. I hoped she had someone to tell her it wasn't her fault. I hoped she felt stronger with each passing day. I hoped that despite everything she didn't give up on the place she called home. Even to this day, I hope she still runs.

Where Melanin Dwells

VINCE ROBINSON (Glenville)

young voices bleed through the silence
of night

hear me
say they

sonic booms
and sparkling dollars
light the sky
through dawn

feel me
cry they

leaving debris
to line the streets of their displeasure

in Glenville
and every other 'ville
where melanin dwells

redlined lead filled
toxic soils lower life expectancies

fresh
takes a back seat to abundant
processed nutrition-less
bodega matter in plastic packages
courting cortisol
causing loss of control

absence of nature
leaves a void in judgement

lack of culture
leads to nonexistent respect

no apology

words
replaced by the cacophony
of scattered explosions
shouting indifference

as the walls come tumbling down
in spectacular fashion
unimagined
until now

no one has the answer
to Marvin's anthem

uncertainty reigns supremely
with the planetary energy
singing its song

change will come
when it comes
and no
sooner

anxiously

normal's return
awaits

Remembering Bobby

GAIL ARNOFF (Downtown)

On the long summer days before camp begins, my best neighborhood friends Lesley and Linda and I head outside right after breakfast, roller skates tied together and flung over our shoulders, bike tires pumped. We're ready for adventures, but most of them only involve excursions to the woods at the end of the street—really, just a vacant lot on a hill overgrown with trees and prickly shrubs—where we play hide-and-go-seek for hours or discuss plans to run away from home when we're much older, maybe fourteen. But in the summer of 1955, we're not prepared for an event more fantastic than anything we could imagine: the arrival of Bobby Avila, star of the Cleveland Indians, who has rented the house across the street from us for the summer. I will always remember the excitement that Bobby and his family brought to us, but those memories are tinged with sadness as well, for the end of that summer and the following fall brought tragedies large and small to me and our street, marking the end of my days of innocent fun and tamping down much of my playfulness and spontaneity.

On the Friday that Bobby and his family move in, the word somehow gets around the neighborhood, and by 11:00 on Saturday morning their entire front lawn is awash in bikes and boys, at least fifty of them. I want more than anything to cross the street, but it's pretty clear to me that this is a boys' only event, and at eleven years old I am not confident enough to confront the boys, who no longer want to hang out with girls. And so I stand on our front lawn taking in the scene and consoling myself with the fact that I live across the street from Bobby Avila and can walk over there almost any time, but just not now.

Not taking time to put down the kickstands, the blue-jeaned, striped t-shirted boys have dropped their bikes on the grass and now mill around in small groups, hands shoved deep into their pockets. None of them move toward the door, and I wonder if they are not quite sure what to do next. Ring the doorbell? Wait until Bobby comes outside? Like pilgrims at Lourdes, they stand in hushed silence, and I do the same, hoping that Bobby will appear.

We don't have long to wait, for within minutes Bobby Avila opens the front door and surveys the crowd. He is not so much taller than the boys, but his body looks powerful: biceps bulge from his white t-shirt, and even from a distance I can see his massive hands. Three little girls and a boy, all copper-skinned like Bobby, open the screen door and stand behind him, peeking out from between his legs. In one arm, he holds a sleeping baby. While he takes in the scene, smiling, the boys stand quietly. Are they terrified that he might order them out of his yard? But Bobby widens his smile and calls out, "Buenos dias, boys! Gracias for the welcome!" Instantly the boys rush toward him, most of them with balls for him to sign. Bobby holds up his free hand and the boys freeze.

"Wait! Wait!" he calls out. "We have a whole summer to get to know each other. Right now it's time to take my kids in for some lunch." A small, dark-haired woman—a slightly larger version of the little girls—steps outside and surveys the scene. She shakes her head, takes the baby from Bobby, and shoos the rest of their children inside.

"Manana," Bobby says, waving the boys away.

The boys return to their bikes, some of them kicking at the tires, others looking back over their shoulder in case Bobby has changed his mind. They silently ride away, a few of them glancing at me. I give them a wave and wonder if Jimmy Brown, who lives on the next street and was my playmate for years, might decide that I am worthy of being his friend again. Sure, I am just a girl, but a girl who lives across the street from Bobby Avila.

My family gets to know Bobby and his family very well that summer. The four oldest kids range in age from three to seven, and they appear at our back door regularly in the morning, usually about 9:00. My fourteen-year-old sister and I are happy to entertain them, give them snacks, teach them English, and pick up a few Spanish words. Playing school has been one of my favorite activities ever since kindergarten, and I am thrilled to have four eager pupils who are much more vocal and animated than the stuffed animals who usually fill in as my students.

The most special days for my sister and me happen when Bobby invites us to a game. My sister spends hours deciding which blouse to wear, which shorts. I am ready in five minutes, decked out in my summer uniform of jean shorts and a t-shirt. When my sister has at last decided on the most flattering outfit and is brushing her hair for the fifth time, we hear a horn honk and race down the stairs, waving a quick goodbye to our mother as we hurl ourselves out the screen door. There is Bobby in his pink Cadillac convertible, top down, motioning us to get in.

"Hello, my lovely senoritas! It is my pleasure to escort you to the baseball stadium." My sister always gets to sit in the front, since she's older. She whips out from her purse a blue and red flowered scarf, covering her head and then dramatically tossing the ends over each shoulder. Then she smiles at Bobby, and I realize that she has managed to put on red lipstick without our mother noticing. In the back seat, feeling like the little sister that I am, I glare briefly at the back of her head, but then turn around and notice some of the neighborhood boys following us on bikes. I wave to them, trying to look as perky as Sandra Dee. The boys scowl and pedal harder, trying to keep up with us. As Bobby peels out of Dysart onto Fairmount Boulevard, I wave once more and, when I am sure that the boys can no longer see me, practice a few air kisses. Then I settle in for the rest of the ride to Municipal Stadium, smiling smugly at people who gawk at Bobby and the car when we stop for a light.

Bobby parks in the players' lot and points us toward the special entrance for families and guests. He gives my sister and me badges with our names. I hang back a little and let my sister lead the way. She takes off her scarf, shakes her pony tail a few times, and prances to the gate, looking so confident and grown up that I wouldn't be surprised to see her take a cigarette out of her purse and ask someone for a light.

In the family section, there are lots of little kids running around, and all the players' wives seem to be blonde, skinny, and beautiful. Not my kind of skinny, with stick-pin legs and flat chest, but what I think must be sexy skinny, with small waists cinched in by wide belts, curvy legs, and full breasts. Even my sister looks a bit intimidated by these women. One of them smiles at us, introduces herself as Early Wynn's wife, and invites us to sit with her and her children.

By the fifth inning, the Indians are losing 6–1. Bobby has struck out once and walked twice. My sister is reading to Early Wynn's kids and I am off in my fantasy world. I may look like an eleven-year-old girl, but in my mind I am twenty-one and being romanced by one of the Cleveland Indians, a man who looks very much like Bobby Avila. Just as we are about to be pronounced husband and wife, I hear my sister calling my name. The game is over, and we need to meet Bobby back at the entrance gate. So close to get married, and now I have to leave that fantasy for another time, which will probably be soon, as I find myself moving more often into that parallel world in which life is more satisfying and interesting than mine. But since I don't know or understand what really happens on a honeymoon—I've heard my sister and her friends talking about it, but I'm sure that what they're saying couldn't possibly be true—it's probably good that I got interrupted.

As the weeks go on Bobby and his family become less of a novelty to our neighborhood, and by August, when we have just a few weeks left before school starts, it is unusual to see even one bike parked on Bobby's lawn. The Indians are still battling the Yankees for first place. We have watched the All-Star Game on television with Bobby making an appearance as the alternate second baseman. My sister starts to spend more time with her girlfriends planning what they will wear for the first day of ninth grade and deciding which boys are the cutest, while I am still playing school with Bobby's kids, who now are speaking half in English and half in Spanish.

Although I am sort of looking forward to being the oldest in elementary school as a second semester sixth grader—I am what is called a "midtermer," which means that I started kindergarten in January—already I start to miss the easy pace of summer. Once school begins, we will be reminded daily that in a few months we will be going to junior high, where much more will be expected of us. I'm not so sure that junior high is where I want to be. One of my girlfriends has already gotten her period, and it's disgusting to think that will happen to me soon. It doesn't seem fair that the boys don't have to go through that mess, and part of me wishes that I could stay eleven and in elementary school a few years longer.

At the end of August the Trenton family, who rented out their house, comes back; Bobby and his family return to Mexico. A few months later Mr. Trenton moves out, leaving Mrs. Trenton and their four children so that he can live with another woman. I'm not supposed to know the part about another woman, but I hear my mother talking on the phone, using the words "divorce" and "tramp." Only one of my friends doesn't have a father at home, but that's because her father died. I begin to worry every time my parents have an argument.

Teddy Schwartz, who is fourteen and lives next door to us, stops pulling down his shade at night, and from my bathroom window I see my first naked boy other than my little brothers. Lesley and Linda, my best neighborhood friends, die in a house fire, trapped on the second floor while trying to get to their babysitter, who is sleeping in the attic. She survives after jumping out a window. I begin having a recurring nightmare in which Lesley and Linda's parents come home to a burning house just as their daughters are being put into an ambulance; it's a nightmare, but it's also what I have seen from our living room window.

For weeks I smell the charred furniture which is pulled out of the house and piled up on the tree lawn.

What has started out as a summer of excitement and adventure has moved into a fall and winter of sadness and worries. The wistful eleven-year-old girl who stood on the lawn on that summer day is gone, replaced by an almost-twelve-year-old who has trouble falling asleep at night. Everything seems to be changing too quickly. A “For Sale” sign goes up at the corner of our woods, and by spring most of the trees have been cleared and a house is nearly complete. Lesley and Linda’s house is repaired, and a new family moves in. I find out some years after the fire that their parents have adopted a daughter, who will be in my class when I student teach ten years later. Mrs. Trenton and her children move to another city.

My parents decide that with four kids we need a bigger house, and when they can’t find one that they like, they decide to build. Although my sister and I get to help design our bedrooms, I am not happy about leaving Charney Road. I complete one semester of seventh grade at Wiley Junior High, but when we move to Shaker Heights I have to start seventh grade again because they don’t have midterm. I don’t know anyone at Shaker, and to make the situation even worse, we only have a half day of classes until the new junior high building is finished. Without lunch period and activities, it’s hard for me to get to know anybody.

Occasionally I still have dreams about the summer of 1955. I see flashes of Bobby Avila, smiling at me with impossibly white teeth and beckoning me to him. As I get closer, I realize that he’s not Bobby at all, but my father. At this point I usually force myself awake. But before I fall back asleep, I try to remember everything about that magical summer: the bike-filled lawn, Bobby’s kids in my pretend classroom, the rides in the pink Cadillac. The rest of the memories I put away for another time.

About ten years ago, Bobby came to Cleveland as a representative of the old Negro Baseball League, which he played in when he was quite young. I wondered if he would remember the summer of 1955 on our street. As I waited in line to see him and studied his face, it looked so familiar to me: the wide smile, the deeply tanned skin. When it was my turn to shake his hand, he looked briefly surprised, and, when I reminded him who I was, he immediately hugged me.

"My little senorita all grown up!" he exclaimed. We chatted briefly and my husband took some pictures. I asked Bobby what he remembered about that summer on Charney Road. He briefly closed his eyes, as if trying to recall some images. Then he took my hand, looked into my eyes, and said, "I remember the kindness of you and your family, how you opened up your home to my little ones. It was a beautiful summer. Gracias."

Before the guard told me and my husband to keep moving, as others were waiting in line, Bobby said softly, almost in a whisper, "A long time ago, so many memories, so many years."

Two years later, I read Bobby's obituary in the paper. So many memories. So many years.

This Too Shall Pass

D. L. WARE (Mt. Pleasant / Buckeye)

Livingston Road, Historic Shaker Square District, Cleveland, Ohio
March 31, 2020—12:10 a.m.

"Oh my gosh Babe! What are we going to do? Do you think they are going to make us all get vaccinated?!" Vimbayi spoke with terrible dread in her voice as the film credits began to roll. Damien and Vimbayi just got done watching the 2011 pandemic thriller *Contagion*, which is a movie about healthcare professionals, government officials, and everyday people living in the midst of a pandemic as the CDC works to find a cure. The movie eerily mirrored the same situation of their real life COVID-19 outbreak. States being placed on lockdown. Curfews were put in order. Social distancing and face masks were mandated. All public spaces and places were shut down. Millions of people were dying. There was a race to discover a vaccine.

"Don't worry babe!" Damien said. "They will eventually come up with a vaccine and it will all go back to normal—just like in the movie." He said with an insecure tone. Vimbayi had already become obsessed with all things COVID-19. She relied on the nightly news reports, where she was always shocked about the increased infection rate and death toll. She made sure that her household stayed packed with all the essentials. The pantry was full of snacks and dry goods. They had plenty of bottled water and canned goods. Their family practiced cleanliness, making sure their children washed their hands as they kept them in doors. They wore latex gloves and face masks in public. She washed her face and hands repeatedly and continuously wiped down all touchable surfaces throughout the house and expected Damien to participate in and enforce the cleanliness and order necessary to keep Vimbayi's phobia at bay. Over the course of the evening, Damien had a few drinks and was a little tipsy by the end of the movie. Kissing his wife goodnight, he realized that his empty minded "just like the movie" response offered no comfort whatsoever. He wasn't sleepy. Damien knew that binge watching movies and TV series about pandemics wouldn't be the best idea. The Ware family's Netflix-and-chill quarantine style made Damien restless.

In the dark, on his side of the bed, Damien held on tight to his optimism, as a family of five experiencing a nationwide lock down. In the dark, the house was quiet and everyone was sleep—leaving him alone in his thoughts as they played out on the ceiling above him. His mind raced between the day's headlines and the fact that the movie was so real. Dwelling on various parts of the movie, Damien placed himself and his family in the various possible scenarios. He thought about the future for his children, Dakarai (9), Garikia (5), and Danayi (3), and their education. At the beginning of the pandemic, Damien and Vimbayi lost both of their jobs. Vimbayi, an administrative secretary with the local school district, was laid off due to schools being closed for the rest of the year. Damien, who is a social worker, was suddenly fired from his job with the federal government for what he believed to be retaliation for whistleblowing on a supervisor. Nevertheless, they had no income, and no one was hiring in either one of their fields of employment. They had no health insurance. Bills and mortgage were steady due. Their savings dwindled by the minute. They had to apply for government assistance and his claim for unemployment was under appeal.

Getting up out of bed, Damien grabbed his glass that sat on his nightstand. The glass had a couple of swallows left. With his glass in hand, he walked over to their bedroom window. Looking past the curtains and into the still dark street, gleaming beneath the rain and the streetlights, Damien remembered his service to his country during Operation Iraqi Freedom and said to himself aloud, "This too shall pass!"

Livingston Road, Historic Shaker Square District, Cleveland, Ohio
March 31, 2020—6:00 a.m.

In an attempt to reinvent their thirteen-year marriage, they dedicated themselves to a healthy living lifestyle. This was an attempt to intentionally focus their energy on coming out of this worldwide pandemic better individuals as a family. Since the pandemic began, Damien and Vimbayi started walking three times day, morning, noon, and night. This calculation was based on Vimbayi's step count needing to be 10,000 steps. She was playing no games about their weight loss journey. The pandemic sets Damien's wife on the journey that has been staring at her in the mirror, living in her waistline since the birth of her child Danai back in 2016.

They try to leave early enough to watch the sunrise break into the day, but because of Mr. Ware's white wine embellishments the night before, it was hard for him to roll out of bed at their usual time. Damien and Vimbayi's living exercise route changed from time to time. Being that they lived on the border of Cleveland and Shaker Heights, it was trickery choosing the most peaceful and serene routes where Vimbayi never felt comfortable or walking the Kinsman or Buckeye route where Damien on the other hand felt right at home. The abandoned homes, vacant lots, excessive morning blight of empty Hennessy bottles, used food boxes and random types of trash—hair weave, condom wrappers, cigar butts—were too unsettling to walk pass at times. On a walk towards Buckeye and Shaker Square one morning, they walked past a bus shelter that had human excrement smeared on the bench and shelter window. A horrible sight that they both couldn't unsee as they vowed never to walk that way again.

The early morning vagrancy for bus fare, a sandwich, or a cup of coffee from people that seemed to be roaming from the night before also made the morning walk unpleasant. On another morning, Damien and Vimbayi walked by what seemed to be a homeless man lying in front of the entrance door of the neighborhood convenience store on 140th street. It was 5:45 a.m. and the store wasn't even open yet. On this particular day, they chose a route that extended from their home on Livingston Road, which is in the Historic Shaker Square District, into the Shaker Heights neighborhoods to Shaker Heights High School, back to their quaint home, settled on the border that separated inner-city southeast Cleveland from the pristine forested streets of Shaker Heights.

"Alright babes, I'm ready when you are!" Damien said coming out of their bedroom's bathroom. Coming into the bedroom—Vimbayi was ready to go, but was preoccupied with News Channel 5's morning report . . .

"Ahmaud Arbery, a black man that was seen investigating a neighborhood construction site, was chased and gunned down by white vigilantes who were father and son . . . *chirp*."

As the report continued on, Damien interrupted the broadcast by turning the TV off, bringing an end to her anxious gaze as they reported about another black man being killed by the hands of systematic racism. "Let's go babe—so we can this morning going!" Damien said, knowing how the news as of late has been a trigger for the both of them. Their daily workout routine and diet released the endorphins necessary to keep them well as they addressed the pressures of indefinite uncertainty. Walking down the steps onto the first floor, the exercising couple walked through the dining room into the kitchen. Since the mask had been acknowledged as a must by government officials, they kept their face masks by the kitchen door leading outside, along with the other cleansing essentials. Baby wipes, hand sanitizer, the small rubbing alcohol pad packets. "Should we wear our face mask?" Vimbayi asked as she reached for her mask shoving a number of rubbing alcohol pads into the breast pocket of her Nike Air Dry-Knit athletic top. "Nah, we should be fine." Damien said, ignoring last night's nightly news briefing about wearing masks while exercising. Subconsciously, Damien always felt uncomfortable as an African American male heeding to the precautionary measures of wearing a face mask. He felt like he was asking for trouble wearing a mask in a neighborhood where the likelihood of being racially profiled was rather high. With the killing of Ahmaud Arbery in Georgia, it was proof that Damien's racial identity as a black male put him at risk of being a suspect of circumstance. "Besides . . ." he added, ". . . I aint tryna be chased and gunned down in front of those million dolla homes for looking suspicious, plus it's hard to work out and breathe in those things!" In response, Vimbayi inhaled and exhaled deeply shaking her head in a silent way. She agreed in saying, "You got a point about the breathing," leaving her mask on the kitchen counter. Grabbing her phone, she set her fitness app to count their steps toward the goal of 10,000 steps per day. They walked out into the morning, locking the door behind them.

Livingston Road and Southington Road, Historic Shaker Square District, Cleveland, Ohio
March 31, 2020—6:20a.m.

Walking up Southington, the sky was early and warm. It's orange and blue colors were inspiring as the light breeze promoted the fresh air to rustle the trailing branches leading up to the high tree top canopy, as Damien and Vimbayi journeyed over the uneven pavement toward Van Aken Boulevard. The green lawns were well-kept and the old towering trees were lush. The birds were chirping and the morning traffic was light, accenting the day's newness as they conversed about the irony of last night's film *Contagion*. "I wonder how much of this will play out like the movie?" Vimbayi asked rhetorically. "In the movie it took them two years to find a cure!" she went on. Damien in response said "Was it that long? I don't think it was that long! We can't be in quarantine for two years; I don't even want to think about that!"

There was light north and south bound traffic of assuming them to be essential workers on their morning commute as Damien and Vimbayi scurried across the Rapid Transit Authority's Blue Line railway, which crossed Van Aken Boulevard. The Blue Rapid transit line holding commuters passed along the tracks that divide the boulevard into the north and south lanes. Coming into the interior of Shaker's Woodbury Neighborhood, their walk continued to lead them up Southington Road. Getting deeper and deeper into the neighborhood, the houses morphed from Colonial style homes into mini mansion both modern and old with large yards front and back. On their walk, Damien and Vimbayi envied the spring breaking in the emerging perennials and the dandelions of some unkempt lawns of houses that they passed. They courteously maintained the social distancing etiquette as they politely stayed away from on-comers. This new route was active with people walking their dogs, jogging, and biking. There were no signs of blight or destitution like in those other directions.

Walking by the Shaker school complex, up Woodbury Road, their pace quickened with their minds removed from the woes of unemployment and viruses and early childhood education. Shaker Heights was known for its large trees and beautiful and antiqued homes, with large yards and unique designs. On their path they came across a home remodeling project that had just been completed. They slowed down their pace so as to marvel at its structural design and the layout of its landscaping. It was a two-story home, made of brick and stone with a long walkway leading to a screened in porch. There was an automatic sliding gate, with a small fountain that was visible through the natural border made of medium sized shrubbery that concealed the backyard. The front lawn was a deep dark green that had automatic sprinklers with a variety of flowers and foliage set professionally. It also had a natural border smaller sized shrubbery that surrounded the front of the home. There were large windows, where through one of them you could see a fancy chandelier hanging in the middle of winding steps at the entrance. It was a gorgeous home.

Moving along, they were headed back home as the lane curved towards Van Aken Boulevard again. They re-centered their focus on the morning walk which was more than halfway done. All of a sudden Vimbayi got inspired to take a workout selfie on her new phone, so to share with her mother and brothers in England. As they paused to position their faces into the small screen of the camera, a neighborhood jogger ran up behind them. Sweat dripping from his brow, he said in panting breathes "Hey y'all! I can take that picture!" the jogger stopped his stride to come in our direction. As he approached jovial and chipper, Vimbayi couldn't help but to think of the nightly news report from the evening prior. Passing the friendly neighbor her phone, Vimbayi heard Lester Holt's voice in her head say, "Exercising without a mask during the pandemic can cause the spread of COVID-19. Due to the droplets of sweat, COVID-19 can linger in the air . . . " As she passed the phone over to the stranger, her face flushed; the brown of her cheeks turned burgundy red as she folded into Damien's arms to pose for the picture. Damien posture began to tense due to the jogger's intrusion, but he went along with it also just to be polite. Before he took the picture, the jogger cleared his throat with a gross and disgusting "haaaaka thoooo," spitting his phlegm to the ground beneath his feet. "Excuse me," he said. While he figured out the camera feature, Damien paid attention to his sweatshirt and pants drenched from his laps around Shaker High School. Vimbayi frowned in repulsion as they looked at each other, ready for this experience to be over. His eyes tightened watching the heat waves of condensation rise from his head, imagining it to be COVID-19 seeping from his pores. The jogger's hair was long, wet and pulled into a ponytail that hung to the bottom of his neck. All Damien could think about was the virus traveling from the joggers infected being to him and his wife. In taking a knee in front of Damien and Vimbayi to position his shot, the jogger thought that the house that Damien and Vimbayi was standing in front of was theirs. "I want to get your beautiful home in the background!" he said repositioning himself at a different angle. The notion of their new makeshift cameraman jogger thinking that the house was theirs changed the body language of Damien and Vimabyi's face and pose. Finding a good spot, the jogger finally called "Ready. Set. Cheese!" enthusiastically snapping the picture. Looking back at the screen, the shot wasn't to the jogger's liking. That's when the jogger motioned to take another picture. Damien stepped up and insisted that his picture taking time was over. "That will be enough, sir! Thank you." Damien said firmly. Off guard the jogger sutured his response "Aaaawwwe—you sure? I didn't get a good view of your home in the picture." Agitated by his persistence, Damien took the phone out of the jogger's hands and said, "That's ok!" again, wiping the phone off with his shirt. Vimbayi recognized the tension in

Damien's action and aura and said, "Thank you, sir, that was so nice of you, but this isn't our home." Face blushing, the jogger then said, "Oh no, I'm sorry. How embarrassin', I should be mindin' my own bidness ntway. Have a nice day y'all!" he said apologetically proceeding to jog along, as if social distancing wasn't a thing.

Walking away from the exchange, Damien and Vimbayi realized how much the propaganda around the pandemic has altered the way they interacted with the world. No longer can they be so willing to allow strangers into their personal space, but the idea of face mask and hand sanitizer being items that you can't leave home without is a concept that should never be taken for granted. "We should get tested ASAP!" Vimbayi's face frowned, wiping her phone down with the antibacterial alcohol pads she stuffed in her pockets at the beginning of the walk. "Calm down. I'm sure we're going to be fine." Damien said in another attempt in offering empty comfort. "What chu mean—you sure?!" Vimbayi was right and Damien knew it. On the rest of the walk, they both stayed to themselves in their thoughts. It was the uncertainty that stayed in the back of Damien's mind. He was uncertain about his family' future. Their healthcare and their children's education. His family had no income and would soon run out of savings. All he had was his health, his family and his love for writing and with that he knew that this too shall pass.

Argos on Lake Erie's Shore

RAY MCNIECE (Collinwood)

for Tim and Arlo

Lake Erie evening, a great blue page
upon which epic lines miles out crest
and disappear, but it is the silence between
surging surf crash washing hush, that swell,
into which the grey bearded man
beside the dying dog stares.

The dog rolls on a dead shad, the man smiles,
the great blue page has turned again,
telling no tale but what the man reads
as alabaster evening sails unfurl
and sunset, which he does not try
to capture on a cell phone, sinks

like a blast furnace on a rusty freighter,
or golden skull ablaze, or Ra's barge,
or burnished shield of Apollo
that only the too few crew sailing back
to Ithaca would know—
it looks like a biscuit to the dog.

The great blue page has turned again,
the same diaphanous azure as the sky
or vice-versa, and he has finally rowed home
to Cleveland, and the dog rolls in death
one more time before huffling up,
turning to look, *are we going?*

Burnt Popcorn

NAIMA OMAR (Mt. Pleasant)

We are drawn outside by realizing that we will not be able to sleep with all the pyrotechnic festivities going on directly behind our home.

"I bet they don't do this at University Circle" proclaims my resident anti-Cleveland and pro-leaving-153rd-Street expert Brandon.

One house has torches in the yard and a variety of things placed on the path directly in front of the house. I don't look closer, although I wonder why they would put so many seemingly random objects on the sidewalk at night. Their dog or cat is assumed missing, and Selena and her male companion go looking for it. Soon the matriarch of the house discovers that the animal has been under something and call them back to the house, "What it is gonna be like when we finally move out of Cleveland?" asked Brandon, hoping to speak his destiny into existence. "Cleveland sucks, that's a fact. These people spent more on fireworks than the city spends fixing potholes. You can't bring a war veteran here."

I never thought about that, but I guess you're right. Of course, not all veterans have PTSD.

Brandon and I watch the fireworks from the porch. They explode from all angles. I can see some reflected in the upstairs windows of the house across the street. Some are behind it and slightly to the right others are far left, perhaps a few blocks over. Some are almost directly behind the house across the street. The burst directly behind the house across the street is mostly purple and white. A few yards down the street, orange and white projectiles threaten to light the porch on fire. Behind my house and to the left, I see a lot of red, green, white, and orange. All are loud, but the ones directly behind my house that I can only see by reflection are the most thunderous. The smell is like burnt popcorn.

At some point, it becomes clear that the random junk on the sidewalk of my almost next-door neighbor's house is, in fact, fireworks—and lots of them. This will probably go on until at least 2 a.m. Some of the explosions shake the house without me seeing where they are coming from.

A woman screams, "That almost hit me!"

Cars go by cautiously. Perhaps my neighbor is a professional. He lights several in a row with a sparkler producing an impressive show. Despite the excitement, we all have our devices. Brandon is finding a place to escape and lamenting that each location has its weaknesses. Texas is too hot. California is too expensive. Florida and Arizona are racist and hot/humid. He takes a break from geographical research to take a few photos; also, he is a rather good photographer. Alex is reading about a sadistic dentist and claiming that Kanye West is running for president.

The fireworks had been going on for a month or a week; it seemed like a month to me. It was a welcome distraction from the neighbors arguing. The second-floor guy complained loudly about the third-floor couples' loud arguments. Even if we couldn't move out of Cleveland, maybe we could find a better house. I had stopped thinking that the girl on the second floor was a prostitute, so what if her friend answers the door completely nude. Just because that guy with the dreads said she was selling ass doesn't mean anything. How can you trust the word of a man who comes to someone's house demanding a bed without even having a vehicle to transport it in? Ok, so the guy she lives with has a fancy car. A lot of folks around here have fancy cars.

The third-floor couple decided to watch the festivities from a friend's car. They look so cute together. No one would ever guess that, a few weeks ago, he broke a window putting her out.

The house across the street with the two American flags has some very appreciative guests who applaud every time my neighbor creates an especially impressive display. I am happy to learn that the guy across the street isn't as lonely as he pretends to be.

We decide to go to bed around midnight, but it is no use. The rumbling continues long after we grow tired of watching beautiful bombs burst in the air. The crazy part about it is fireworks are supposed to be illegal. Real crime over the holiday weekend precludes anyone from worrying about the thousands of unauthorized pyrotechnics shows occurring all over the city.

2050

ANITA R. TOBIN (Glenville)

A marginalized dream
Another lifecycle.
My home place
30 years in the not so distant future.
A neighborhood will grow
A call to its multifaceted heritage.
As proud as we are now
We'll be just as proud then
Thumping pulse of the city beneath our feet.
Beats on the streets of my neighborhood.
We produce career prodigies
Mathematics, science, music, writers and athletics.
A picture of joyous unity.
A well rounded environment built from rubble
Blood will no longer stain the streets
Fathers and Mothers will no longer be ripped from the arms of the ones they love
For non-existent crimes and misdemeanors
We will be the free radicals
As we approach the precipice
New age mentality
Lessons from the renaissance will reign
As we ring out
EQUAL RIGHTS
FAIR ACTS
CONSCIOUS THOUGHT
Minds full and bodies prepared
Ready to fulfill their purpose
New freeways
Bus transport through the city
Seamless
2050
Glenville will be so pretty.

VII. Cleveland Is What We Offer in Our Words

Rememory St.

TIERRA LATRICE (Fairfax)

The breeze is my good friend
She meets me during the hours where
The sun shows no remorse

My street isn't a quiet one
But it will fool you in some moments

Stories live here
Lively
Sad
Fearless

The house two doors down
Holds 4 generations
More on the way

The house just across
2 little girls greet summer mornings
Screaming laughter
Joy

Just a glance
You couldn't tell of any pain
Loss

No
Not on this street
Not at golden hour
Not from my porch
Not through my eyes

The sidewalk
Just a path to you

A memory
To me
Where the wheels of my first bike (bratz)
Left skid marks after taking off on the 14th or 16th try

The driveway
The home of my first owned car
Dori

The gunshots at night
Oh, that?
That's just the sound of America
Nothing to do with my street

There's a tree
I'm sure took root
The day my parents brought me home

A house they built in persistent love
A home I'm sure was awaiting my arrival
My destiny

The house to my right
A 100-year-old woman lived

I remember her husband
I remember their love
Together perched on their porch

I wonder
Who this street was to them
What their lives were like
What they loss on this street

Before the house
Built in persistent love
Before my homecoming

Sometimes I count the cars
How many cars have I watched pass by
My life
What were they doing
When I laid in my lilac bedroom
crying
Where were they going?

Blindfolded
I could still walk every step
My legs know
What my eyes can't see
So does my heart

This house
This street
My life
My journey
One

One whole being
Inside the other

Built in persistent love
Awaiting my arrival

My only soul remnant
Soul reminder
Of him
Loss

I remember the doorbell ringing
And the dog

Who's dog?
Your dog
But where are
you.

Our parents
Their faces
I couldn't read
The longest night of my life
The night I couldn't leave the porch
The night I couldn't feel myself breath

But
The breeze
The wind
My good friend
While pondering life without him

A brother
A street
A home
The anecdote to my life

A breeze

When she blows
I can remember
things
My soul won't let me forget

Remember my roots
Remember my loss
Remember

The home built in persistent love
My home
On this street
With the wind
As my good friend

Immigrant Churches on The Near West Side: St. Theodosius

JAMES ZAFEROPOLOS

(Tremont / Ohio City)

The steel mills hunker down to sleep
like surly beasts at rest after the hunt and kill,
blinking and yawning in their sweet satiety.

They drift off soundly, like the simple innocents they really are,
sleeping more soundly, surely, than the ones upon whose lives
they nightly sup; and as the demons rest, lost in the satisfactions
of their darkling lair, they feel the curving backbone of
their sleeping mates beside them in the dark, and snore
in ultimate contentment.

They all sleep well, deep in the brooding valley
that we call The Flats, where we don't ever dare to go.

The beasts are satisfied with life
                                        because
they have that molten metal flowing white inside them,
like the blood of immortality.

They cough and belch, spewing their acrid smoke and glowing steam
into the gasping sky. They know too *well* how to torment the lungs
and sear the souls of men who cannot rest in peace beneath
their belching stacks.

They drive men's spirits deep into a troubled sleep
with such dark images of Hell on earth as only Bosch
could have imagined in another time and place.

Yet, still, St. Theodosius in her grandeur stays.
The old church stands her ground.
Her tarnished onion dome rises above the crumbling
neighborhood, a proud green presence by the grace of God.
The immigrants who built this place and worshiped here in former years,
longing to see in her even a vestige of their home-place lost, *o lost*
to them forever more, those immigrants have long since gone to their reward,
if not back home, and now, only the poor and the displaced reside within the shadow of her onion dome.

They cling in tenuous abandon to this thing they call a life,
clinging tenaciously to hope, along the crumbled streets and alleys
of the neighborhood, in tenements the city built,
commonly called "the projects" here about, which cling like stubborn weeds
onto the crumbling hillside where the trash discarded there
is all the neighborhood must use to keep itself from tumbling down
into the Flats below. Yet, still, St. Theo's tarnished onion dome remains,
an anchor rooted stoutly to the ground, to keep the whole securely in its place.

Steadfast. Protector. Guardian of abiding hope.
The unacknowledged symbol to the people living here today,
Of what it means to stay, and to survive.

West 116th Street

MICHELLE SANDERS (Edgewater)

He knew I lived on the second floor
in a small closet apartment on West 116th Street
that night
I opened my door and ushered him in.

kindness worn with the flash of large
gold chains
encrusted with diamond-like naivety.

It felt familiar and so did he
And I thought I knew him.

But I couldn't have known him

I grew up with five brothers in a Detroit bungalow
Where I learned that some men aren't kind like
my brothers
They take what they want and tell you that you
wanted it in one smooth motion

This man, I let into my home
used manipulation
Like baseball cards from the '80s
And gaslighting was his MVP pick.

I knew better.

I thought I knew better.

I thought I knew him but that night, I learned
That my female body was never human to
some.
That my female body belonged to him because
to be a woman is to be a

A trinket

A trophy

A toy

That night I gave him shelter
Because he said he was in need

And I

I should have listened to my gut
I should have created better boundaries
I should have
I could have

I wish I could have wished myself back to that
Warm urban bungalow in Detroit
With my brothers
Because West 116th Street at the far end
where the Starbucks on the corner
touches Clifton
in this Cleveland neighborhood

Doesn't feel like Home

The last bit of love I had for Cleveland died that
night
In that neighborhood on West 116th Street
In my small closet apartment
As he held my wrists as tightly as this
neighborhood grips my lungs
making it harder and harder for me to
breathe

1910 West Boulevard

LEON MICHUAD (Cudell)

The red maple stands solemnly,
Silent witness to the kill,
Of a kernel's final journey,
Not yet 5,000 dawns fulfilled.

For one last shaken moment,
A day's dream ended abruptly.
The grace of light will never foment,
This seed's life-circle thusly.

O'er my shoulder is reflected,
Against mirrored windows laid bare,
The massive memorial collected,
To honor Tamir's spirit here.

A child's hopes will only bring,
That which imaginations allow,
To our own Young Black King,
And the name we will avow.

Never realizing the resultant rigor,
Of how our privilege protected,
Another pulling of the trigger.
And, yet, the future will be affected,

By today's silence, it would seem,
To neutralize one more child's dream.

Cleveland Smells Like Hope Today

ERIN DOLAN (University Circle)

A day
When the weather feels like
Love itself
Sunshine smiles in my eyes
As I drive down the Shoreway
Living for its breeze
I have just dropped off
Borrowed bones
Feathers and fur
Whole birds even
At the place my nephew calls
The dinosaurs' house
Then gathered my strength
To return to work
I have a habit
Of holding my breath
Even before this temporary era
Of collective breath-holding
I keep it
Pulled back
Somewhere
Between my shoulder blades
Like when I think
If I just wait
Long enough
And sit
Still enough
I will see Steggy move
Plates serving sunshine
Twinkle in his eye
Or her eye

I don't know
How do you know
With a stegosaurus
And I don't mean to put a gender
On an inanimate object
That is replicating
An animate object
The life-size stegosaurus
Outside
A museum on a circle
Of museums
Where my circle has met
For
Years
Another circle
Art museum trips with babies
Heart walks with birthday buddies
Merry-go-rounds with my sister
That one time
Cleveland starts here
Says the sign
And so did I
Well
Not really
I was born somewhere else
But here
Is where I found myself
Here is where I keep coming back to
Came back crying
Came back smiling
Came back around
Like that circle of museums

Full of history
And art
And painted ponies
Where Cleveland starts
And
I ended
Up

Ode to Lake Erie

MICHAEL LODERSTEDT (Collinwood)

Erie darling, you've pulled me
here, my Atlantic, my Ellis
Island. Your brothers, sisters
seemed indifferent, dumping
God knows what into your vastness.
Diving deeper through the green
pea soup of bricks and tile, of algae
cauldron of midges yet to rise
their swirling clouds hovering
over roaring freeways.

Three winters now, you no longer pull
your thick white blanket. Instead flinging
lace curtains across the trees, furiously
chewing your edges, tumbling oaks
and sycamores alike, rounding
them into bleached bare bones.

> Oh Crib, tiny orange period
> to end city's sentence, filler
> of coffee pot, water pitcher.
> We're made more of you
> than you of us.

Some nights I dream you'll take
me from this house, the kitchen
cabinets strewn wreckage, we'll cling
to anything left floating, the dishes,
glasses becoming polished pebbles. Look--
there's an old Euclid Beach marble
sand blasted smaller, an agate moon.

Gonna Leave Me Walking on the Riverbanks

HERBERT ASCHERMAN (Cleveland)

I was bereft and burning, I was on fire inside
I was vacant and hollow, part of me had died
I walked the endless river, it was dirty and black
Like the nighttime clouds overlooking the Flats
Where the fire of steel mills lights the midnight sky
And the smoke of fortunes falls on passerby's
Now the nights are cold along the riverbank
I've got no one near me, no one else to thank
For the missing days and the days that aren't
While the time goes by for a burning heart

Gonna leave me walking at night on the banks of the Cuyahoga
Gonna stare into that endless water
Time just seemed to do what it oughta.

Nothing much I can do except watch the open sky and breath in the lake winds
That come raging down from Canada, slicing cold across the eerie beach

Something always reminds me
Of the life I never lived
I made my choice with no regrets, not one
Just another day like this, another day like this, another day like this
Me and the river just flowing, just flowing to the end

Time on the beach walking on the frozen sand
Time I should be doing, doing what I can
I couldn't make up my mind
I floated away along the river, along the river
Just walking on the water, along the river

I thought I knew, I thought I knew what was real
It was the water, it was water made me feel
It was the water, it was water made me feel
Burning, with the fire bright, the river lit the Cleveland night

What was it, where it was, that burned so deep inside of me?
Where's the source and strength in the fires of thought
And the fires within?

It would ever be the constant, be the river's flow
Be the burning of the moment, that would light my soul
Walk along the river. watching every step
Pockets full of hands, lips with cigarette
Held the match to my face, like the river's flame
Another hour or day it always seems the same
And the burning inside me never disappears
It's the glowing of an ember fed by glowing fears.
Ain't no angel gonna hold my hand.
Ain't no devil by my side.
Just the barking of a stray dog on the river be my guide

Sundown on the Cuyahoga, watch it fading away.
Gonna leave me on the riverbanks to walk another day...

Burning alone
Burning inside
Yeah...

Neighborhood Memories

BRENDA BEY (East 55th)

I begin my "historical" journey on Euclid Avenue at the junction of East 105th. I am standing in front of the Alhambra Theater, remembering that my mother took me and my brother there to see *The Wizard of Oz*. It had probably been released some fifteen years or more earlier. Just west of the Alhambra is the Keith Theater, which I recall as a landmark and nothing more. Across the street—south and slightly east—is the Fanny Farmer candy shop, which holds an unfulfilled chocolate dream. And around the corner on a side street is the SS Kresge five-and-dime. Looking down that street puts me in mind of a forbidden other world.

My historical footsteps lead me to the University Theater near East 107th Street. I am a preteen come to see *The Ten Commandments*. It is here that I experience my first encounter with a sexual predator: "his" hand is under my dress before I am aware of it. In my silent trauma, I get up and leave and tell no one. Why didn't I scream? The magic of the East 105th and Euclid area is now dark and unappealing.

I'm standing in an historical space. I don't have a timeline to share, just bits and pieces of memories. There is an indoor market at East 55th and Woodland, with its huge clock that can be seen for miles, or so I imagine. Produce is brought in from the shipping yards near where I live on 45th Street off of Woodland and where I learn to cross the tracks of the train yard at around six or seven years old.

Milk is only twenty-five cents a quart at the grocery store downstairs from my Aunt Freda's apartment which I visit sometimes. It is also where I live for a short while—5019 Woodland—and where I last see my father alive. I'm not allowed to cross Woodland Avenue, but one day I do and I get in trouble for agreeing to get a stack of newspapers for the downstairs store proprietor. I am not yet seven years old. I wonder if my "father"—Big Syl—had a conversation with the store proprietor or if I alone suffered the consequences.

At times, I see the conductors of the streetcars get out and put the cables back on the lines that give it power to travel the streets; I can see this from above looking out the window of Aunt Freda's apartment and sometimes while I am a passenger on the streetcar with my mother. We travel downtown and then back to 5019 Woodland; no farther.

I learn to swim at the POC community center around the corner from Aunt Freda on 55th Street. In that same community center, my mother earns the title of City Swim Champ during her teenage years. It's near the Majestic Hotel, where Black celebrities come and hangout. As a young woman, my mother works there. In the afternoon after school, I sit on a stool at the bar and it's alright with me and everybody else. I don't know what my mother sees at other times, but I think it is the reason she squashes my excitement about becoming a singer. In short time, she moves across the street to work at the Log Cabin. From both locations, she puts me on the bus. I pay the eight cents fare, and she instructs the bus driver to let me off at Cedar Avenue so I can go to my ballet and tap lessons at the Phillis Wheatley Association. Maybe I walk down Cedar from 55th to about 45th. Or maybe I take another bus; transfers are three cents. I'm six years old, I think.

My life is concentrated in a changing neighborhood. I'm living in the midst of dilapidated housing on East 45th street. There are other children there; Ms. Glover cares for us all. My mother visits on occasion. There are holes in the floor under the tub and rats climb out. They get caught in rat traps and we take them to the trash in the backyard. I learn to go to the bathroom at night without fear, but my brother doesn't, which may explain his bedwetting. We finally leave that place now that I am seven-and-a-half and my brother is four-and-a-half. My mother tells us that Big Syl has died. My brother is Little Syl. I'm nobody, except, I look like my mother. Big Syl is actually not my father. We drive off with my mother and Morris, who takes on the role of stepfather. Where are our clothes, our belongings? What happened to the bicycle that was stored in Aunt Geraldine's attic next door to Ms. Glover?

I now live with my mother and stepfather, Morris, on East 70th Street and go to Giddings Elementary. At night we listen to Bishop Sheen while Morris sleeps—my mother works nights as a barmaid—and unconsciously learn the introduction to the Catholic Rosary, because that is what is broadcast on the radio and repeats over and over—"Hail Mary, Full of Grace, the Lord is with thee. Blessed art thou among women, and blessed is the fruit of thy womb Jesus . . ."

My footsteps pace streets and sidewalks that hold harsh and confusing memories. They have me seek an escape. And I wonder: does no one else see what I see, hear what I hear, know what I know? My neighborhood memories do not overflow with joy and laughter. But I dig into the past and mine scenes and experiences that can be quilted into a memorial tapestry. And I now realize that there is more to be remembered, more to be said and eventually, more to appreciate and release.

Where I'm From

MYSONIA SHORTER-LITTLE (Collinwood)

After George Ella Lyon

I'm from hot combs on the stove,
from the scent of Fabuloso and Pine-Sol on Saturday mornings.
I'm from Barney and princess bed sheets repurposed as curtains
and the matching pillowcase as halloween candy bags.

I am from Euclid Beach,
the local treasure of peace and celebration.
The forest, beach, summer festival, wildlife friends and family reunion destination
all in one.

I'm from something always getting broken
and no one ever did it
I am from train tracks and potholes
whom I dodge like a hurdle while ghost riding my bike before the streetlights came on

From Malcolm X and Assta Shakur,
strength and resilience.

From "you're the oldest, act like it"
and "stay in a child's place"

I'm from Baptist church on the holiday and Catholic school during the week
Where the Bible held manifestations and financial blessings

I'm from Kim's and China Mountain
From licking Kool-Aid and sugar from my palm

From my mother's survival skills and my father's charm as a defense mechanism

My aunt's glass table as the official symbol of becoming a teenager

Family photos on the mantel shelf along obituaries
or along the wall adjacent African art
Where under the mattress was the bank and safe
I'm from making a dollar out of a dime and making it a good time.

Making it

STEVEN PRYCE (Downtown)

My dad encouraged me
to go into sales
So I worked for free
at his growing company
It was cheaper than
a master's degree

I saw it as a path to white collar work
I had never even been a sales clerk
But I jumped in the game
And tried to make a name for myself

I sent out my marketing letters
But commission salesman wanted to do better
I was left with whatever

It still looked good for an internship
And I landed a job in downtown Cleveland
It was a daily one-hour trip

The office was in the Galleria Tower
My boss had a polite, southern accent
I was sure he was transferred
That it meant success

Within months, I was paranoid and depressed
I couldn't control what I was thinking
My career was surely sinking
So I quit, as my dad would suggest

I returned to Cleveland for treatment
So I could still work locally
I still like to think about what I could be

Blue Collar Cleveland

S. RENAY SANDERS (Collinwood)

The Titans of Industry
Still, hold court on the bridge
Over the once burning river
Where steel mills shot fire in the sky
And billowed smoke from their stacks.

Early risers to all night third shifters
Went to work
Metal lunch boxes in tow
Hard hats, steel-toed shoes, blue collars
Working Joes with names displayed on their shirts.
Hot molten steel being tended to by muscular men
Never in need of a gym.

Now industry is about tourists
Museums, casinos, and posh eateries.
Rock n Roll has been encased
In a pyramid of glass
Glistening on the lake.
Music archived and digitized.

But the raucous rock in roll's roots remain
Played in the taverns, honky tonks
and neighborhood saloons.
In the past on payday
The railroaders, stevedores and factory Joes
Ordered up boilermakers or perhaps a glass of POC
With a blonde, brunette or redhead standing by
Jukebox blaring
polka, country or maybe a bit of the blues.
The women and the music
a reflection of the neighborhood
In which they were raised.
The heart of rock n roll was and is in Cleveland.

The sons and daughters of the hard-working Joes, hustle
To answer the call of the new industrialists
Dealing cards, waiting tables
Serving the connoisseurs and conventioneers
Who speak of the comeback of this town.
Truth is she never left
Cleveland survived your insults
Rust Belt, mistake on the lake
Didn't much care what outsiders thought anyway
But hey welcome to Cleveland
Enjoy your time here and in her spirit
Rock on!

Contributors Notes

Fatimah Abouelsoud *(Larchmere)*
Fatimah Abouelsoud graduated with a degree in neuroscience from CWRU and seeks to build a bridge between art and science with her writing. The growth of her twenties has been shaped by her community, spirituality, and nature.

Pamela Anderson *(Steelyard)*
Pamela Anderson's poetry has appeared in a number of online and in-print journals (*Jenny*, *Whurk*, *Atticus Review*, and others). Her new poetry chapbook—*Just the Girls: A Kaleidoscope of Butterflies; A Drift of Honeybees*—was released in August 2020 by The Poetry Box Press.

Shelley Andrews-Hinders *(Detroit-Shoreway)*
Shelley Andrews-Hinders is an author, poet, artist, singer, musician, activist and spiritual seeker dedicated to envisioning a new world order where all are free to pursue their best possible selves without fear of retribution. She is the author of *Medium Brave: How a Transgender Woman Overcame Years of Self-Inflicted Conversion Therapy and Found True Happiness*, from Page Publishing.

Gail Arnoff *(Downtown)*
After thirty years as a teacher in the CMSD, Gail Arnoff began teaching at John Carroll and Case Western Reserve. When she is not teaching, writing, or reading, she is running, practicing yoga, gardening, baking, and doting on her six grandchildren. Her memoir pieces have been published in *The Persimmon Tree* and *Lilith* (online). "Remembering Bobby" is about a Cleveland summer which began as exciting and fun, but ended with sadness and a goodbye to childhood.

Herbert Ascherman *(Cleveland)*
Herbert Ascherman is a fourth generation Clevelander. He is a lifelong professional photographer, published author, literary journal editor, educator, historian and collector.

Leslie Kouba Bednar *(Jefferson)*
Known for her quick wit and loud laugh, Leslie Kouba Bednar is a high energy force with an intense interest in all things not boring. Currently, she

is a multi-career professional. Under her own business name, LLBednar Consulting, LLC, Ms. Bednar provides engagement consultation to help small to medium size nonprofits grow their target audiences. In April 2018, she earned her realtor's license and currently works with Howard Hanna. Recently, Ms. Bednar became a Reiki Practitioner, Master Level and provides energy wellness feedback through private consultation. Her love of good words and clear communication supports her favorite activity—thoughtful conversation. In her free time, Leslie enjoys doing jigsaw puzzles, sitting on her new deck with a cool beverage, and playing with words, especially to produce memoir writings and humorous essays.

Brenda Bey *(East 55th)*
Brenda Bey lived on the East Side around 45th to 55th off of Woodland. She has lived in Cleveland all of her life (seventy-one years) and this writing "assignment" has allowed her to unpack memories she didn't know were still present and able to be accessed. She has dabbled in creative writing and poetry and the writing required to support her messages as a speaker.

Toneisha Black *(Hough)*
Toneisha Black is a twenty-three-year-old nursing student. She was born in Mt Sinai Hospital four months early and remembers her mom and cousin telling her how small she was. She was raised near Hough on a street called Holyrood and lived there until she was twelve. She lived for the block parties as kid and loved seeing her neighborhood coming together.

Jeffery Bowen *(Edgewater)*
Jeffrey Bowen is an accomplished poet, journalist, and Afro-Cuban percussionist. He has performed with multiple jazz, folk, R&B, reggae, and roots music ensembles, appears on several recordings, and serves as the resident conga player, percussionist, and spoken word artist with the popular Cleveland band, Cats on Holiday. His poetry has been published by *Art Crimes*, *Cicada*, *Cool Cleveland*, *Crisis Chronicles*, *Dimensions*, *Doan Brook Watershed*, *Excursions*, Green Panda Press, *Hessler Street Fair*, *Off the Page*, Procrastination Press, Poet's League of Greater Cleveland, *The City*, *The Cleveland Reader*, and *Whiskey Island Magazine*.

Marcia Camino *(University Circle)*
Marcia Camino holds an MFA in Creative Writing from the University of Alaska, Fairbanks. She is author of *Crayzee Aayzee: A Poetry Abecedarian*; *Oomee Boomee, Space Yogi*; and *The Pink Lotus Yoga Professional and Yoga Teacher Training Program Manual.* From 1996 to 2003, Marcia lived, studied, and worked in Little Italy and University Circle. She currently lives in Avon Lake.

Rose Carter *(Larchmere)*
Rose Carter has lived in Shaker her whole life. She moved to this area two years ago because of the Larchmere Arts District. She chose this neighborhood for its inspiration, sense of community, and safety. She wrote this poem while sitting outside on her steps while observing how different the people of this community move due to the pandemic.

Bruce Checefsky *(Hough)*
Bruce Checefsky was born in Jessup, Pennsylvania. He attended Kutztown University and received his master's degree from Cranbrook Academy of Art in photography. He is author of several film scripts and numerous short stories. His critical essays have appeared in magazines and art journals both here and abroad. His stories depict human vulnerability as he examines themes of identity and intimacy. He is recognized for his detective-like abilities to follow strangers and investigate people's private lives. He is currently is writing a novel. Checefsky is recipient of a CPAC Creative Artist Fellowship and three Ohio Arts Council Individual Artist Excellence Awards in photography and film. He is a four-time recipient of CECArtslink International Fellowships. His films and photography works are in the permanent collections of the Cleveland Museum of Art, Akron Art Museum, Museum of Modern Art NYC, Whitney Museum of American Art, Brooklyn Museum of Art, Allen Memorial Art Museum, The Minneapolis Institute of Arts, The Jane Voorhees Zimmerli Art Museum, and others.

Lisa Chiu *(Asiatown)*
Lisa Chiu is a Taiwanese American writer who often covers family, food, culture and community. Her work has appeared in *McSweeney's*, *People*, *Ohio Magazine*, the *Plain Dealer*, the *Mercury News* and anthologies including *Cheers to Muses: Contemporary Works by Asian American Women* and *Who's Your Mama?: The Unsung Voices of Women and Mothers*.

She is passionate about collaborative creative projects. In 2012, the Asian American Women Arts Association selected her for its Emerging Curators Program, and she conceived and developed Hungry Ghosts: Yearning for Fulfillment, an exhibition in San Francisco featuring thirty-eight visual and literary artists. In 2017, one of her essays was featured in *Crossing Borders: Immigrant Narratives*, a staged reading held during the Cleveland Humanities Festival.

Carolyn Cooper *(Glenville)*
Carolyn Cooper was born and raised in Cleveland, Ohio. She is a graduate of the Cleveland Metropolitan School District, and earned both her bachelor's and master's degrees from Kent State University. She still resides on the east side of Cleveland and represents the Glenville neighborhood.

Victoria Davis *(Larchmere)*
Victoria Davis is a writer advocating for literacy, wellness and education for all.

Matthew Dettmer *(Gordon Square)*
Matthew Dettmer is a physician living and working in Cleveland. He has been an active member of Literary Cleveland since 2018.

Danielle Dixon *(Mt. Pleasant)*
Danielle Dixon is a published author, poet and artist. She is a current Baldwin House writer in residence. She has a BA in Visual Art from Kent State University and is an alumna of The Cleveland School of the Arts. Her work has been published in *Cleveland Stories Volume 2*, *Inclusion Magazine* and *The Luna Negra*. She currently lives in Cleveland, Ohio.

Erin Dolan *(University Circle)*
Erin E. Dolan is a teacher, actor, playwright and poet based in Northeast Ohio, and a member of Literary Cleveland. Her works have been performed at Talespinner Children's Theatre, Cleveland Public Theatre, The Illusion Factory and Spark Theatre 4 Youth. She is also a member of Stratosphere, a Northeast Ohio–based artists' co-op. Erin is fiercely proud to be a Clevelander, and especially revels in all of the art that is created here.

Jo Donofrio *(Detroit-Shoreway)*
Jo Donofrio is a freelance writer, editor and marketing professional. Her work has been published in various outlets including *Cleveland Magazine, The Plain Dealer, Guideposts, Old Brooklyn News, MD News,* and many more. In addition to her writing, Jo teaches an "Effective Writing for Business" workshop at Cleveland State University and is an Adjunct Instructor in the MBA program at Southern New Hampshire University.

Meghan K. Donovan *(Detroit-Shoreway)*
Meghan K. Donovan is a writer and visual artist. By day, she is a legal secretary at the Cuyahoga County Prosecutor's Office. She is a member of the board of Cleveland Peace Action and volunteers at All Faiths Pantry and with the Alliance for the Great Lakes. She has been active with Cleveland Pandemic Response. She has a bachelor's degree in English from Baldwin Wallace University. Her current project is a novel about hacker nuns in the 1980s. She lives with her wife and fur-children in the Edgewater neighborhood.

Susan Eyerman *(Detroit-Shoreway / West Park)*
Susan Eyerman is a life-long Clevelander. Along with her husband, she raised her family in their current home, their "starter" home in West Park. Her early years were spent in the Detroit-Shoreway neighborhood near St. Malachi. She fills non-work hours researching and creating stories, gardening and cooking, and loving life in Cleveland.

Lola Farron *(Buckeye-Shaker)*
Lola Farron began writing about eight years ago. She enjoys writing poetry, creative nonfiction and memoirs. She spent many years teaching elementary school/ the creative arts and practicing Occupational Therapy. Lola's father was a Hungarian immigrant and he owned a shoe store on Buckeye Road. She worked in the store with her entire family. Lola witnessed the transition of the area from Hungarian to integration with the African American community. Her pastimes include: love of the arts, holistic health and global cuisine.

Joshua Fye *(Jefferson)*
Joshua Fye is a graduate of Cleveland State University in Social Work and has been involved in supporting Cleveland's communities for over five years. He and his wife live in the West Park neighborhood of Cleveland

with their two cats and one dog. He enjoys spending his time in the city's local coffee shops and metro parks

Mark Gilson *(University Circle)*
Mark Gilson is a retired nurseryman and former CPA with many fond memories and work experiences of Cleveland.

Joanne Lozar Glenn *(Union / Miles)*
Joanne Lozar Glenn is a freelance writer, editor, and educator whose work has been published in *Beautiful Things (River Teeth), Peregrine, Under the Gum Tree, Ayris, The Northern Virginia Review, Brevity*, and other print and online journals.

Karen Gygli *(Collinwood)*
Karen Gygli grew up in Collinwood near Waterloo Road in a duplex with her mom, dad, brother, sister and grandmother. She is an Associate Professor of Theater in the Department of English at John Carroll University.

Barbara G. Howell *(Downtown)*
As a writer and international educator, Barbara G. Howell loves coming home and relishing the wealth of international programs like the ones from Cleveland Council on World Affairs which brings professionals who become friends to homes and neighborhoods all across the city.

Victoria Johnson *(Union / Miles)*
Victoria Johnson is a published and award-winning poet. She published her first book in 2005, her work has been printed in over twelve anthologies, and she will release her second book early 2021. Living in the inner city of Cleveland, Ohio, she is a retired teacher and her husband is a retired inspector for the City of Cleveland. They raised their two children in the inner city. Both of their children went and graduated from Cleveland Public Schools. In November they will celebrate their fortieth wedding anniversary as high school sweethearts.

Kate Bigam Kaput *(Cleveland)*
Kate Bigam Kaput is a seasoned writer, editor, and freelance journalist based in Tremont. Originally from Cuyahoga Falls, she spent seven years on the East Coast before returning home to Northeast Ohio and making it her mission (and passion) to show the world that Cleveland

does, in fact, rock. She blogs at GreatestEscapist.com and can be found on various social media platforms as @katekaput.

Annmarie Kelly-Harbaugh *(Near East)*
Annmarie Kelly-Harbaugh is the author of *Here Be Dragons: A Parent's Guide to Rediscovering Purpose, Adventure, and the Unfathomable Joy of the Journey*, a memoir about the sweet and wonderful misery of raising children with someone you love. She lives in Cleveland, Ohio, with her husband, three kids, and a marshmallow dog named Higgins.

Paul Koszkalda *(Detroit-Shoreway)*
Paul Koszkalda is 62 and grew up on West 69th and Bridge Avenue. He has lived there for thirty years. He went to the Cleveland Public Schools where he learned drafting as a trade. He is still employed in that field. He got married in 1984 and they lived upstairs of his childhood house until 1988.

Sujata Lakhe *(Ohio City)*
Sujata Lakhe was born in India and grew up in steel-town Bhilai before immigrating to Cleveland in her early twenties. She has one master's degree in Botany from India and another in Molecular Biology and Microbiology from Case Western Reserve University. She has worked as Molecular Biologist at Cleveland Clinic and MetroHealth Medical Center. She has lived most of her adult life in the Greater Cleveland area. She has co-authored research papers in peer-reviewed scientific journals. Presently she has stepped away from laboratory research, and she would like to transition to science writing. She speaks and writes Marathi and Hindi in addition to English. Her interests include reading, yoga, Kathak dance, travel, nature (esp. plants), and photography. She cares about social justice issues and is concerned about women's functional participation in our society and our natural resources stewardship. She likes to write personal essays, creative nonfiction, short stories, and hopes to write a memoir. She presently lives in Chagrin Falls, OH, with her husband William G. Barnard IV, daughter Samira Reddy and a Pit Bull Terrier named Luna.

Tierra Latrice *(Fairfax)*
Tierra Latrice grew up and lived in the Fairfax neighborhood for over twenty-three years. A graduate of the Cleveland School of the Arts with a major in theater, she went on to graduate from Kent State University with

a bachelor's degree in both Journalism and Digital Media Production. Currently, she works as a Marketing Associate, however her true love and passion lives in storytelling. She launched her first blog this year, PageWorthy, where she publishes her personal essays and articles meant to inspire healing and trauma particularly for women of color. It's her life's desire to write work that inspires and heals. She chose to continue to grow in her craft and treat life as a journey to be explored.

Michael Loderstedt *(Collinwood)*
Michael Loderstedt is a near thirty-year resident of the North Collinwood "beach streets" where he's refurbished an old summer cottage and built a studio. He loves this neighborhood next to Lake Erie, a quiet community nestled within the city. He also runs Photocentric, a contemporary photography gallery in the Waterloo Arts District. He is a retired art professor from Kent State University, now concentrating on his writing and studio work. He received a 2019 OAC Fellowship for Non-Fiction for a draft of his memoir *The Yellowhammer's Cross*. His visual work is held in the collections of the Cleveland Museum of Art, the Akron Art Museum, Progressive Insurance and the Cleveland Clinic and many others.

Dominic Mathew *(Ohio City)*
Dominic Mathew is an architect-planner who works to address workforce mobility and job-access challenges in Northeast Ohio with an economic development collaborative. He came to Cleveland in 2018 and resides in Ohio City.

Ray McNiece *(Collinwood)*
Ray McNiece is the author of nine books of poems and monologues, most recently *Love Song for Cleveland*, a collaboration with photographer Tim Lachina and *Breath Burns Away, New Haiku. The Orlando Sentinel* reporting on Ray's solo theater piece "Us—Talking Across America" at the Fringe Festival called him "a modern day descendant of Woody Guthrie. He has a way with words and a wry sense of humor." He toured Russia with Yevgeny Yevtushenko, appeared on *Good Morning, Russia* and performed at the Moscow Polytech, the Russian Poets' Hall of Fame where he was dubbed "the American Mayakovsky." He has toured Italy twice with legendary beat poet Lawrence Ferlinghetti. He fronts the blues rock band, Tongue-in-Groove. He was appointed Poet Laureate of Cleveland Heights in April 2020.

Leon Michaud *(Cudell)*
In 1995, Leon Michaud moved to Northeast Ohio with his wife, and their young son. Over the subsequent years, his family (which now numbers five) has enjoyed experiencing life in the inner-ring community of Euclid. Living in this effervescent echo of the rich cultural tapestry of the Cleveland neighborhoods, has provided local exposure to numerous facets of a global society. During his career, he has engaged in various roles as an electrical engineer, while, artistically, he has always enjoyed playing music and singing (having even composed 'some tacky ballads' in his twenties.) He seriously began writing poetry three years ago at the age of sixty-two. At the time he felt drawn to the positive power of words. As his speaking voice can sometimes lose control of the message, he takes comfort in knowing that his written words are predominately a clearer and kinder oracle for communication. As he starts to gravitate from the role of working "stiff," he looks forward to more quiet time to pursue messages that he believes merit attention.

Maria Miranda *(Edgewater)*
Born and raised in Cleveland, Ohio, Maria Miranda (they/them) is a queer, radical feminist, and nonprofit professional committed to advancing reproductive justice. For more than fifteen years, they have worked in the social sector in various roles including health advocate, fundraiser, grantmaker, and community organizer. Maria has advocated for women's lives by devoting time and money to various social justice organizations including NARAL Pro-Choice Ohio Foundation and New Voices for Reproductive Justice. Creatively, they have written works for the stage and have dabbled in performance art. Maria earned a bachelor's degree in Political Science and Women's Studies from Eastern Michigan University, a master's in Public Administration from Villanova, and a Certificate of Advanced Studies in Public Policy from Northwestern. In addition to working full-time in philanthropy, Maria teaches courses in Women's and Gender Studies and nonprofit topics at the collegiate level. Maria's idea of self-care is taking naps, enjoying fried foods, drinking gin, and watching *The Golden Girls* daily.

Denise Monique *(Glenville)*
Denise Monique resides in Glenville with her husband and children. She is a graduate of Cuyahoga Community College, Cleveland State University, and Case Western Reserve University. Denise is a licensed social worker

and loves to travel as much as possible. Each year, she travels to a place she has never been before. Other hobbies include reading, sometimes as much as a book a day. Growing up, Denise often won the libraries summer reading club recognition for having read the most books. Her nickname was One-Hundred due to her educational efforts. Her dad gave her his own nickname of Squirrel, as she was a tomboy, growing up, and could be found in a tree most days. Denise Monique is the author of *Despite My Odds: A Memoir*, which was released earlier this year.

Charlotte Morgan *(Glenville)*
Charlotte Morgan is a journalist and writer based in the historic Glenville neighborhood. She teaches at Cleveland State University and sometimes leads workshops for Literary Cleveland.

Debbie Morris *(Near West)*
Debbie Morris writes personal essays, poetry, and short fiction. She has participated in writing workshops through Lit CLE and Cuyahoga County Library. Debbie has also been involved with the Skyline Writers Group monthly critique workshops and was chairperson of the Annual Skyline Writers Conference in 2011 & 2012. She holds a bachelor's degree in Business Communications from the University of Phoenix. Debbie works at Case Western Reserve University in the Mandel School of Applied Social Sciences as the Assistant to the Director of Lillian and Milford Harris Library. When she is not writing or managing the library, Debbie enjoys spending time with her family.

Nailah Muhammad *(Mt. Pleasant)*
Nailah Muhammad has lived in the Cleveland area for almost fifteen years. She has a degree in Human Services and is currently pursuing a bachelor's degree in Journalism. She is a playwright, storyteller and slam poet and has performed on many stages across the country. She is currently in the process of publishing a book of poetry that will be completed and released this fall.

Bill Newby *(Cleveland)*
Bill Newby enjoys using poetry and prose to record, reshape and reflect upon daily experience. His work has appeared in *Whiskey Island*, *Bluffton Breeze*, Ohio Teachers Write, Palm Beach Poetry Festival's Fish Tales Contest, *Blue Mountain Review*, *Panoplyzine*, *Sixfold*, and three Island Writers' Network

anthologies. He was a 2018 Pushcart Poetry Prize Nominee, and his first collection, *Sea Chests or a Carry-On*, is available from Amazon, and a second collection, *Passing Through*, will be published soon.

Naima Omar *(Mt. Pleasant)*
Born in Atlanta, GA., Niama Omar moved to Cleveland at the age of five. She attended AJ Rickoff, Robert Fulton, Riverside and Gracemount Elementary Schools. She earned an Associate Degree in specialized technology from Pennsylvania Culinary and Bryatt & Stratton College. She also has two children.

Davidione C. Pearl *(Near West)*
Davidione C. Pearl is a published journalist, novelist, musician and multi-disciplinary artist with work focused primarily on global and domestic socio-political and eco-political issues. Raised in Shaker Heights, he currently resides in Ohio City.

Mimi Plevin-Foust *(Shaker Square)*
Over her career, Mimi Plevin-Foust has been a poet, glass artist, screenwriter and filmmaker with an M.F.A. in Dramatic Writing from NYU. Mimi's poetry, screenplays and articles have been published by *Carve Magazine*, *Fourteen Hills*, *LearnVest/Forbes.com*, *POZ Magazine*, and more. In 2017, she won the Gordon Square Review Poetry Contest for her poem "On the Anniversary of the Kent State Shootings." After living in New York City and New Jersey for many years, Mimi moved back to her hometown of Cleveland where she shares a 106-year-old house with assorted Airbnb guests and her husband, daughter, and cats.

Geoffrey Polk *(Kinsman)*
Geoffrey Polk grew up in Cleveland, where he writes, plays jazz saxophone and clarinet, and teaches literature and composition at Lorain County Community College. He attended Berklee College of Music and received an MA in creative writing from Cleveland State University. He was editor of the literary magazine *Whiskey Island*. His poems and fiction have appeared in *Cobalt Review*, *Brilliant Corners*, *Voices of Cleveland*, *Context South*, *Black River Review*, and elsewhere. Nonfiction publications include articles and reviews on literature and music as well as interviews with David Foster Wallace, Ken Kesey, Studs Terkel, and others.

Susan Poole *(West Park)*
Susan Poole is a mother, lawyer, nonprofit executive, breast cancer survivor, and aspiring author. She is a graduate of Lakewood High School, Baldwin-Wallace College and the University of Buffalo School of Law. She left the practice of law to raise her three children, all of whom are now young adults, and several of Susan's essays about parenting have been featured on the popular website *Grown and Flown*. Susan is finally at a point in her life where she can also follow her passion for writing fiction—romantic suspense to be exact—and she has recently completed her debut novel, for which she currently is seeking representation. She and her husband currently live in Avon Lake.

Leslie Price *(Lee-Harvard)*
Leslie Price a native Clevelander who has fantasized about writing since childhood watching her photojournalist father read, write, and take photographs for the *Call & Post*. She finally has the time to pursue her dreams full time of author and artist. A graduate Capital University with a degree in Biology, Leslie developed her career from the laboratory, to pharmaceutical sales and marketing, retiring in 2017. Her first job while attending Beaumont School was at the famed Hough Bakeries in Cleveland. Leslie attributes her patriotism, work ethic and tenacity to her parents who instilled the American dream into her spirit, growing up in the Lee Harvard area, watching those around her pursue their goals of homeownership, working hard and fighting for equal rights during the Civil Rights era. Currently working on a novel, she writes to encourage, uplift, and inspire others to overcome life's challenges through introspection and self-love with resilience and courage to reach one's purpose of self-actualization and fulfillment.

Steven Pryce *(Downtown)*
Steven Pryce has always liked writing and won The Ambler Literary Award from Hillsdale College. He has also had brief jobs as a journalist. Currently, he is a member of Literary Cleveland and The Writers Group in Akron.

Sonya Pryor-Jones *(Glenville)*
Sonya Pryor-Jones was born and raised in Glenville. She is a mother, wife, and educator currently living in South Euclid, Ohio. Sonya is the Founder of Fab House, a community based digital fabrication lab and expert-in-residence program for the Glenville neighborhood.

Erin Radigan *(Warehouse District)*
Erin Radigan is a marketing professional living in Cleveland, Ohio. In her free time, she enjoys spending time with family, writing and practicing yoga.

Karim Ragab *(Little Italy)*
Karim Ragab has lived in Little Italy since November of 2019 and has been at work on his craft for many years, now. He has publications in *Vine Leaves*, *Street Speech*, the *East Side Daily News* (a contributor), and the *JJ Outre Review*. He has three novels written and is attempting to query agents in order to publish the first of them. He is currently at work on a fourth novel, entitled *Lovers*.

Vince Robinson *(Glenville)*
Vince Robinson is a writer who has lived in Glenville for the past twenty-eight years. He has been writing poetry since high school and his first writing class at Kent State University in 1975.

Michelle Sanders *(Edgewater)*
Michelle Sanders is a Detroit native who has been living in Cleveland for nine years. Professionally, she works as a Technical Fashion Designer for a local company within the city. In her free time, she writes and creates art that examines ethnicity, trauma, and introspection.

S. Renay Sanders *(Collinwood)*
S. Renay Sanders learned to love the spoken word amidst a family of storytellers, secretly writing her own stories as poems. She came out of the poetry closet in 2010 with a poem in the *Hessler Street Poetry Anthology*. She subsequently had poems published in a variety of anthologies. Her first chapbook *Dancing in Place* was recently published.

Karen Shepherd *(Glenville)*
Reverend Karen Shepherd's family moved to Cleveland from West Virginia in the early '60s and settled in the Glenville area. She loved the library as a child. Her fondness for libraries continues to this day. Reverend Shepherd attended school grades 1-12 in the Cleveland Public Schools, Ursuline College (BA), and John Carroll University (M.Ed). She began her thirty-five-year teaching career as a Language Arts teacher in the Cleveland Public Schools (now Cleveland Municipal School

District). She taught there for four years, subsequently moving to the Warrensville Heights City School District for the next thirty-one years. Karen started her ministry path during the last ten years of her career, by first becoming a Licensed Unity Teacher (2007) and an Ordained Unity minister in 2014.

MySonia Shorter-Little *(Collinwood)*
With generational roots in the area, MySonia Shorter-Little was born and raised in Cleveland, Ohio's own Collinwood neighborhood. She attended Collinwood then finished her high diploma marching at Shaw High. With determination and drive running through her veins, MySonia went on to obtain a bachelor's degree from Central State University and a master's degree from Savannah College of Art and Design. After securing her academic accomplishments in 2017 she came back to the Collinwood area to advance her community through sharing her education and experiences in the city that raised her. Little did MySonia know Cleveland still had much to afford her. Over the last three years MySonia has participated in a plethora of community action activities, taught at various schools in the area and most importantly learned just as many lessons as she has taught along the way. As MySonia continues to advance both herself and her community, she is beyond excited to share with the world and of course with Cleveland what's to come next!

Lindsay Smith *(Tremont)*
Lindsay Smith is a social worker who lives in the Tremont neighborhood. She wrote Lincoln Park Love Letter as an ode to the neighborhood central gathering place. Lincoln Park is special as it brings the community together and provides the opportunity to enjoy nature in the middle of the city. Lincoln Park is a safe haven no matter a person's age, race, or background. It's a place to gather for festivals, picnics, and farmers markets. Its calming presence is always available for all to enjoy.

Kimberly Steele *(Near West Side)*
Kimberly Steele (pseudonym Kim The B-word Poet) is a Poet, Short Story Writer, and Journalist from the East Side of Cleveland, Ohio. She has published clips in the *The OdysessyOnline*, *Gay People's Chronicle*, *TheLetterOnline*, *The Fence Magazine*, and Cuyahoga Community College's "The Voice". She also has poetry in Youngstown State University's *Penguin Review*, Cuyahoga Community College's *BreakWall Literary*

Journal, and 2003, 2005, and 2006 Hessler Street Fair Competition booklets. In addition to these credits, she sporadically publishes clips in Cleveland State University's *The Vindicator* and *BiWomen Newsletter*.

Andrew Sykaluk *(Downtown)*
Andrew Sykaluk is a graphic designer with a passion to help others. He is currently writing a memoir about his family and his late brother Kenny Sykaluk.

Constance Sylvester *(Shaker Square)*
In 1984, Constance Sylvester and her husband moved into a lovely duplex in the Shaker Square area. Four years later, their then three-year-old son became ill and was diagnosed with lead poisoning. They did not know what to expect or prepare for. This has led her to record these events in hope that any family facing this dilemma will have information to better face the situation.

Stuart Terman *(Kinsman)*
Stuart Terman is a physician, previously Assistant Clinical Professor/ Ophthalmology/Case Western Reserve in his home city of Cleveland, married, and blessed with 4 grown children. He was on the surgical/ Ophthalmic surgery staff of the Cleveland VA Hospital for a number of years. His ophthalmology practice in Maple Heights, and then Solon, in addition to being privileged to be on the staffs of the old St. Alexis Hospital, Meridia Southpointe, and SVCH, until he retired. He's had publications in the *Annals of Plastic Surgery*, the *Annals of Ophthalmology*, *The Ohio Family Physician*, *Glaucoma Today*, *EyeNet* (the American Academy of Ophthalmology monthly journal) and the *Consultant for Pediatricians*, among a number of others over the years.

Anita R. Tobin *(Glenville)*
Anita R. Tobin is a Cleveland poet, born and raised in the Glenville neighborhood. She began writing at the age of eleven years old. Her passion is education through hip-hop culture. She attended Ohio University in Athens, Ohio, and graduated with a degree in African-American Studies, Women's Studies, and Sociology. She currently resides in Austin, Texas, where she continues to work on her passion projects with her longtime organization Hip Hop Congress. Cleveland lives forever in Anita's heart as she continues to work within nonprofit and hip-hop culture.

D .L. Ware *(Mt. Pleasant / Buckeye)*
A community-based poet and writer, D. L. Ware is a literacy advocate and literary artist from southeast Cleveland, Ohio. His poetry is on display throughout the Buckeye Corridor and is a regular teaching artist with Literary Cleveland. Husband and father of three boys, Damien finds the act of writing to be healthy and therapeutic and makes time to write daily.

James Zaferopolos *(Tremont / Ohio City)*
James Zaferopolos is a retired professor of history. He was born in 1946 in Northern Greece, of a refugee Anatolian-Greek family. His father died when he was one, and his mother and he came to America in 1955. Except for a stint in the military, he has lived in Cleveland ever since. He has been writing since his boyhood in Greece. At seventy-four, he is just now making an effort to publish. To date, this constitutes a handful of pieces in a couple of journals. Nonetheless, the struggle continues.

About this Book

Founded in 1869, Cleveland Public Library serves the residents of Cleveland through its network of 27 neighborhood branches, the Main Library downtown, Public Administration Library at City Hall, homebound delivery services, and mobile services to daycare and senior centers. From a collection of 10.5 million items, the Library lends over 5 million items a year to its 330,000 registered borrowers and to 43 other CLEVNET-member libraries in 12 counties across Northeast Ohio. Cleveland Public Library is home to the Ohio Center for the Book and the Ohio Library for the Blind and Physically Disabled, serving all 88 counties in the state of Ohio. For more information, visit cpl.org.

Literary Cleveland is a nonprofit organization and creative writing center that empowers people to explore other voices and discover their own. Through an expanding roster of multi-level classes, workshops and events, Literary Cleveland assists writers and readers at all stages of development, promotes new and existing literature of the highest quality, and advances Northeast Ohio as a vital center of diverse voices and visions. For more information, visit litcleveland.org.

Acknowledgements

Neighborhood Voices was made possible by Cleveland Public Library in partnership with Literary Cleveland. Special thanks to program coordinators Christine Howey and Matt Weinkam at Literary Cleveland and Aaron Mason at the Cleveland Public Library. Much of the writing in this anthology was created in free, online summer workshops taught by instructors Stephanie Ginese, Jason Harris, Philip Metres, Darlene Montonaro, Vince Robinson, and D. L. Ware. Thank you for mentoring writers and helping shepherd this art into the world. We're grateful to Anne Trubek, Dan Crissman, and everyone at Belt Publishing for publishing the print anthology, and to Nate Mucha, Alex Catanese, Sarah Kula, and the whole team at Each + Every for designing the website anthology.

CPSIA information can be obtained
at www.ICGtesting.com
Printed in the USA
LVHW052354221220
674915LV00032B/1278

9 781950 843374